brain games
for preschoolers

contents

First published in Great Britain in 2004
by Hamlyn, a division of
Octopus Publishing Group Limited,
2–4 Heron Quays,
London E14 4JP

Copyright © 2004 Octopus Publishing
Group Limited

Distributed in the United States and Canada by
Sterling Publishing Co., Inc.
387 Park Avenue South
New York, NY 10016-8810

ISBN 0 600 60968 5

A catalogue record for this book
is available from the British Library

Printed and bound in China
10 9 8 7 6 5 4 3 2 1

contents

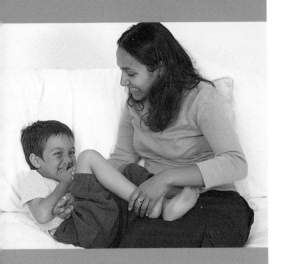

introduction

Experience matters, especially the experiences we have as small children. Providing a loving and nurturing environment for our children is one of the most important things that we, as parents and caregivers, can do. A nurturing experience early in life may increase a child's IQ, it will almost certainly build his self-confidence, and it will often give him a head-start at school. But more important than any of these, it will cement the bond of love and respect between parent and child. Those who play together and so share exploration, discovery, laughter, fun and learning (for that is what play is) have a special bond of friendship. The glue of attachment that bonds a child to his caregivers is strengthened when parents and children play together.

Play is fun, and learning through play allows a child to learn in the natural, relaxed way that suits him best. Enjoyment provides the optimal arousal state – excited enough to learn, but not so excited that he is over-awed. With your support and gentle guidance, a small child can feel confident enough not to give up at the first hurdle.

The child you cradle in your arms in the first weeks of life looks like a miniature person, but his mind is far from fully formed. A new-born baby's brain is only about a third of the size of an adult brain and there is a lot of neurone (brain cell) growth still to come and millions of interconnections between neurones yet to be formed. The parts of the brain that control 'vegetative' processes, such as breathing, digestion and sleeping,

'As psychologists have shown many times, the nature of the attachment formed between a child and his parent permeates all aspects of his early life and provides the model for later social relationships. Research also confirms that parents are usually the child's best teachers.'

are already mature, but the areas of the brain associated with perception, action, learning and memory are far from mature. In the next few years, a child's brain will first race and then, slowly but surely, walk towards maturity.

Experience has an influence on how the brain matures. This can be shown by the fact that the brains of individuals who lack the right stimulation may not mature in the same way as the brains of those who do have that stimulation. For example, we know that the brains of kittens with squints in the first months of life never develop the binocular driven-cells in the visual cortex that normal kittens have and that, as a consequence, they do not have binocular (3D) vision. Children who have squints in the early years of life do not have binocular vision either – although no one has actually looked at their brains, we can assume that they have a similar problem. To develop normally, the cells of the visual cortex must receive an input from each eye. We also know that rats who are raised from weaning in solitary confinement (which deprives them of play) have a thin cerebral cortex compared to socially reared rats. In rats, as in humans, the cerebral cortex is the area of the brain that is associated with perception, action, learning, memory and thought.

Lack of stimulation has implications for brain development, but that does not mean all stimulation is good. Care should always be taken to fit the activity to the child's personality and to his current mood. Some children are more cautious than others, and there are times when all children hate change. Some

'**Play is fun, and learning through play allows a child to learn in the natural, relaxed way that suits him best.**'

love high levels of excitement; others like peace and quiet. Bear this in mind and personalize the games in this book accordingly. Remember, too, that the ages given here are guidelines – children mature at different rates. If an activity says 'from 2 years', and your child still enjoys it at the age of 6, so be it. If he is having fun and still seeks out the activity, he is still learning.

Last of all, remember that if children are pushed too hard by their loved ones, their only option is to switch off. Ambition must come from within. It is always better to attract a child to an activity because he cannot resist it than to push him into it so he cannot avoid it. If he does not want to play the game today, leave it. There are lots of tomorrows.

time
to talk

Talking – and listening – to your
child helps to bring you closer together.
Talking is not only essential for good
communication but is also linked to
effective reading and writing. The games
in this chapter will give you lots of
ideas for sharing rhymes and stories,
developing your child's imaginative
skills and introducing letter
names and sounds.

finish the song
from 2 years

Let your toddler join in with his favourite rhymes.

- Choose a nursery rhyme or song that your child likes.
- Start to recite it, but pause at the end of the line to allow him to finish it: '... All the King's horses and all the King's men... (couldn't put Humpty together again)'.
- Eventually, see if your child can recite the whole rhyme.
- For older children, do the same thing with a favourite story, such as The Three Little Pigs: 'I'll huff and I'll puff and I'll... (blow your house down).'

find a rhyme
from 3 years

Can your child think of a rhyming word?

- Think of a word, such as 'box', and ask your child if he can think of another word that rhymes with it.
- If he finds this difficult, give him a clue. For example, say: 'I know a word that rhymes with "box" – it's an animal with a long bushy tail.'
- When he has found a rhyme, let him think of a new word for you.
- See how many rhymes you can think of for just one word, for example, for 'box', you could have 'fox', 'socks', 'locks' and 'clocks'.

RESEARCH SAYS

'Rhymes train children to hear the little sounds that make up words.'

Research suggests that children who are exposed to rhyme in preschool years have fewer problems learning to read, and this is particularly true for children who have a propensity for dyslexia. Dyslexia tends to run in families and causes difficulty in reading, although it is often accompanied by problems with spelling. One symptom of dyslexia is difficulty hearing a rhyme. Rhyming practice in the preschool years can reduce later problems.

spot the word
from 4 years

Which word from the list rhymes with the 'master' word?

- Tell your child you're going to say a 'master' word, and that you want him to shout out if he hears you say another word that rhymes with it.

- Start by saying, 'The master word is "house".' Then, list several other words, including one that rhymes with house, for example, 'flower, hat, chimney, mouse and book'.

- Your child may shout out as soon as you say 'mouse'.

- If he doesn't, repeat the list, emphasizing the word 'mouse'.

- Vary the game by finding words that start with the same initial letter sound as the master word, such as 'b' for 'ball' and 'baby'.

RESEARCH SAYS

'Small children can only hold one or two things "in mind".'

Research shows that adults can keep about seven things 'in mind', whereas a small child can only keep one or two. This is why children speak in short sentences and find it hard to compare things in more than one dimension. For example, they can categorize by colour *or* shape but not by colour *and* shape. Describing and discovery activities help to stretch their capabilities.

colour search
from 2 years

Can your toddler match the colour?

● Show your child an example of a colour (or, if she knows the colour names, let her choose one for herself).

● Go on a colour search around the house together to find as many items of that colour as you can. For red, you might find a red brick, a tomato, a red pepper, a crayon, a toy car and a boot.

● Make a display of all your objects and talk about how some are toys, some clothes and some food.

● Can your child think of any other red things that are not in your house? Perhaps a strawberry or a red umbrella.

how does it feel?

from 3 years

Encourage your child to use and understand 'describing' words.

- Without your child seeing, put a selection of different-textured objects inside a pillow-case, bag or box, for example, a hairbrush, a pine cone, a pebble, a sponge, a sieve, a feather and a shell.

- Describe an object and invite your child to feel inside the container to find it. For example, 'Can you find something smooth and hard?' (the pebble).

- If she can't find the right thing, give her another clue, such as 'It feels heavy and a bit cold'.

- Older children could describe an object for you to find.

follow the trail

from 3 years

Learning how to follow spoken directions is fundamental to a child's development.

- Hide a small toy or book where your child can reach it.

- Explain that she can find some 'treasure' if she moves exactly as you tell her.

- Put a red sticky dot on the back of her right hand and a blue one on her left.

- Describe each movement in precise detail, using the dots to help your child. For example, 'Walk towards the door', 'go up the stairs', 'turn right (red hand)', 'walk along the corridor', 'open your bedroom door'.

- When she's in the right room, give some false trails first, such as, 'Look under the bed', or, 'Peep behind the curtains'. Then, give the true directions and praise her when she finds the treasure.

13

talking on the phone

teach your child how to use the phone effectively and politely

Young children are fascinated by telephones, especially mobiles.

This isn't really surprising, as we adults often spend time talking, listening, laughing and even crying on them. Children want to be part of the action too, and knowing how to use the phone politely and effectively is a useful practical skill.

At around the age of two, your child is likely to be saying approximately fifty words, though she'll understand many more. She'll already enjoy hearing someone saying hello on the phone and asking her if she's having a nice time – though chances are she'll only nod in reply! As her speech improves, her conversations will gradually become more two-way, though you may need to remind her that the person on the other end of the line cannot actually see her – she'll need to describe in words that picture she's holding up for Daddy to see.

Once your child reaches the age of four, you can begin to teach her how to answer the phone. Suggest she starts by saying

'As your child grows up, she'll want to make calls herself. Tell her that she must always ask you if it's OK first.'

'Hello' politely and asking who's calling. If she doesn't know the person, she could say 'I'll get Mummy'; if she does know the person, she might say 'It's Alice here', and perhaps have a quick chat before passing the phone to you.

As your child grows up, she'll want to make calls herself. Tell her that she must always ask you if it's OK first. If you say yes, she should introduce herself by saying 'Hello it's Alice here. Please can I speak to Katie?' If her friend isn't there, she could leave a short message, such as 'Could you tell Katie that I called?' Explain that using the phone costs money, so calls need to be kept fairly short. Use a timer to show your child when her conversation should end!

play and learn

toy phone

Pretend to call your child on a toy phone, making a 'Brring, brring!' sound. When she answers say 'Hello, is that Alice? It's Mummy here, calling to ask what you'd like to play this afternoon'. Encourage her to reply, then finish by saying 'Great, that's settled, then. Goodbye, Alice'.

out of sight

Ask your child to draw a picture secretly. When she has finished, let her describe it to you, over the toy phone, without saying exactly what it is. Can you guess what she has drawn? Then, swap roles and see if your child can guess what you have drawn from your description 'down the line'.

my first mobile

Make your own toy mobile phone by painting a small cardboard box silver and drawing on a screen, number grid and buttons in thick black felt-tip pen. You could even stick a small picture of a family member on to the screen area and pretend it's a video mobile.

15

things I like...
from 2 years

What things does your child like – or dislike?

- Choose a category such as fruit, colours, toys or games.

- Ask your child to think of three things he likes in that category. For example, for fruit he might say 'I like bananas, pears and mangoes.'

- Repeat with three things that he doesn't like in the same category. For example, he might say 'I don't like oranges, melon and grapefruit.'

- Do the same thing for yourself, explaining why you like and don't like your choices. For example, 'I like yellow because it reminds me of sunshine.'

my feelings
from 3 years

Help your child to understand and express his emotions.

- Tell your child that you're going to think of something that makes you feel happy.

- Name the thing and say why it makes you feel good. For example, eating an ice-cream because it tastes delicious, or sniffing a rose because it smells lovely.

- Ask your child to name something that makes him feel happy – perhaps a friend coming round to play, or making a big splash in the bath. Encourage him to explain why it makes him feel good.

- Repeat the game with other emotions, for example, things that make him feel sad, surprised, giggly, frightened, excited or even cross!

RESEARCH SAYS

'Forming categories is difficult and demanding and needs plenty of practice.'

Baby's brains are not fully formed. The areas associated with 'vegetative' activities, such as breathing, digestion and sleeping, are mature at birth, while those associated with thinking, reasoning and remembering develop in the early years of life. Practice makes perfect and that is certainly true for forming networks of neurones (brain cells) as well as the behaviour these networks control.

our family
from 4 years

Drawing a family tree will give your child a sense of structure.

● Take a large piece of paper and, at the bottom, draw a circle for each child in the family.

● Ask your child to draw pictures of himself and his siblings inside each circle, or he could stick in photos, if he prefers.

● Draw two more circles just above the children for Mum and Dad, and also for any favourite aunts and uncles. Let your child draw pictures in these circles, too.

● Draw a top row of four circles for your child's grandparents, and ask your child to draw pictures here as well.

● Finally, write everyone's name underneath their picture circle.

RESEARCH SAYS

'We are more likely to learn when we are alert than when half asleep or over-aroused.'

Too much stimulation is not conducive to learning, but on the other hand neither is too little. Having fun and laughing raises our level of arousal without pushing us into the fear zone, and so does being exposed to a moderate amount of novelty. For this reason, games which may seem silly as well as surprising variations on old themes help to put children into the optimal learning zone.

I wish...
from 3 years

Let your imagination run wild and make fantastic wishes!

- Start by expressing a silly wish yourself, such as 'I wish we could fly home from the park in a hot-air balloon'.

- Then, ask your child if he can think of a silly wish – the sillier, the better.

- Turn the game around and think of things you don't wish. For example, 'I don't wish I had to eat worms for breakfast every morning'.

- You can use the game to spark off conversations with your child, perhaps about hot-air balloons or what you normally eat for breakfast.

what if?
from 4 years

Giving a favourite story a new twist will challenge your child.

- Read (or tell) your child a story he knows well.

- When you have finished it, go back to some key points in the plot. For example, the moment when Cinderella loses her shoe at midnight, or the bit where the three bears find Goldilocks asleep in Little Bear's bed.

- Ask your child what might have happened if Cinderella hadn't lost her shoe, or the bears hadn't spotted Goldilocks.

- See if you and your child can devise a whole new ending for the story.

rainbow magic
from 4 years

What's at the end of your child's rainbow?

- Draw a rainbow on a big sheet of paper, leaving a space on either side.

- On one side of the rainbow, your child can draw a picture of himself (or you could draw one for him).

- On the other side, he can draw something special he would like to find 'at the end of a rainbow', for example, a chocolate cake or a puppy dog.

- If you can, listen to *Somewhere Over The Rainbow* from *The Wizard of Oz*.

19

making friends

*good social skills are a great asset –
even when you're only three!*

Almost from the moment your baby is born, she will start to acquire social skills, and these grow and mature as she does, particularly as your toddler begins to play alongside other children.

It's usually at around the age of three – often coinciding with the time she starts to attend a nursery or playgroup – that your child will really begin to make friends of her own. You can help your child to become someone whom other children like. Firstly, develop her confidence by talking and listening to her in a way that shows you really value what she is saying. Secondly, teach her good manners – knowing when and how to say 'please' and 'thank you', and how to share or wait for her turn shows consideration for other people. This kind of politeness also helps children to feel safe and relaxed with each other.

When children come to play at your home, show your child how to encourage a new friend to join in an activity. For example,

> **'If you can, invite children to play at your home, and show your child how to encourage a new friend to join in an activity.'**

you could say 'This is Beth. She'd like to play tea parties with you. Can you find her an extra cup, Holly?' Or suggest other friendly opening phrases, such as 'Do you want to play our game?'. Being sociable is also about showing through body language that you'd like to get to know a new person by turning towards her, making eye contact, and smiling in a welcoming way.

Good friendships are based on trust, so it's well worth talking to your child about 'big concepts', such as generosity, playing fairly and being kind. It's often much easier to do this through a third party, such as a storybook character (see below), than with real-life situations that directly involve your child!

play and learn

villains and heroes	teddy's first day	role-playing baddies
Read a story with an obviously bad villain or a classically good hero or heroine, such as *Snow White* or *Little Red Riding Hood*. Discuss the character's behaviour and ask your child whether she thinks it is good or bad, and what she would do in the same circumstances.	Pretend that her teddy is starting nursery school and act out the sorts of things he might say to the other toys in order to make friends with them. Ask your child what sorts of things Teddy might say that the other toys wouldn't like.	Try being an imperious, demanding queen, or a mean, cross witch, and ask your child to explain to you how to be a nicer person. You may be surprised at how much she already knows!

RESEARCH SAYS

'The areas of the brain associated with short-term memory are among the last to mature.'

We know that using a particular part of the brain encourages its development – for example, areas of the brain associated with finger-tip touch are larger in blind people who read using Braille than in blind people who have never learned Braille – so stretching a child's working memory capacity (as these tasks do) can only be beneficial!

true or false?
from 3 years

Can your child differentiate between fact and fiction?

● Tell your child that you're going to say something and he has to tell you whether it's 'true' or 'false'.

● For three-year-olds, make the statements as simple as possible. For example, 'Your name is Ben', 'Dogs go quack, quack' or 'You like bananas'.

● For four- and five-year-olds, make the statements more challenging. For example, 'A cat has two legs', 'The sky is blue', or 'Wheels are square'.

● Give lots of praise for the right answer – and a second chance for an answer that's wrong.

mad sentences
from 4 years

Create crazy sentences and have fun playing with words.

- The aim here is to make a sentence that sounds fine, but doesn't really make any sense. Start off with your own mad sentence. It could be something like 'The giggling kangaroo liked to dance in shorts', or 'My talking dog eats chunky chips for breakfast'.

- Then ask your child to make up a mad sentence. If he finds it hard, help by suggesting a few opening words.

- For an older child, make the game more difficult by saying he has to include words that rhyme. For example, 'The fat bat fell splat on the mat', or 'Louise eats cheese on her knees'.

what's different?
from 5 years

See if your child can spot the words that have changed.

- Explain that you are going to say two similar sentences, but that there will be a slight difference. Can your child spot what has altered?

- Start with something simple, such as, 'The grass is green' and 'The grass is pink'.

- Once your child has understood and become adept at spotting simple differences, move on to more difficult pairs of sentences, such as 'I have two eyes' and 'I have blue eyes'.

- See if your child can make up some sentences for you to spot the changes.

duck's journey
from 3 years

Let your child add sound effects to your stories.

- Start a simple story: 'Once there was a lonely little duck'.

- Carry on with, 'One day she went for a walk – all on her own. Before long, Duck met Hen. "Hello," said Hen, "I peck seeds and I go (let your child say 'cluck, cluck') – can I go with you?"'

- Continue with, '"Of course," said Duck. And on they walked together.' Add more animals in the same way.

- To end, say: 'Suddenly, Duck came to a big field. "What shall I do now?" she asked. "Play a game with us!" cried all the animals. Now Duck wasn't lonely any more.'

mini story
from 5 years

Think of three things and make them part of a story.

- Let your child think of three things at random, for example, a dog, a bag and a biscuit.

- Then, make up a story together, incorporating these things. You could start by saying 'Once there was a dog who found a bag by a bus-stop.'

- Your child might add 'The bag smelt very good, so the dog put his nose inside and discovered a big biscuit.'

- You might say 'The biscuit looked so tasty, that the dog quickly ate it all up.'

- And your child could finish off with 'And then a very cross lady chased him all the way home!'

RESEARCH SAYS

'Small children find it hard to keep track of the sequence of events.'

This difficulty is because the hippocampus – the area of the brain that processes such information – is one of the last areas to develop. Stories help, and making sure that your child is involved in the stories is a great idea.

story round
from 5 years

This game is best played by two or more children – with everyone adding a new layer to the story.

● Start off with an exciting opening, for example, 'One dark and stormy night, a small wizard banged fiercely on my front door. "Help!" he said, "I'm being chased by a terrible..."'

● Your child then takes over. For example, she might say '"...troll, who eats small wizards for his dinner. The only way to stop him is to..."'

● The next person adds another bit, for example, '"...sing him his favourite song, which is..."', and so on.

● Carry on the round until the story reaches a natural conclusion – or until it gets out of control!

25

reading labels and signs

*the 'need to read'
is all around us*

Just take a look around and you'll see how much we depend on labels and signs every day.

We need them on tins and packets to tell us what's inside, on shops to show us what's for sale and on the roadside to give instructions and tell us where we're going. Signs are everywhere, and learning to decode them is part of growing up.

With very young children, you can point out simple visual signs that convey vital information. At home, taps usually have red or blue marks on them to indicate whether the water is hot or cold; jam jars have pictures of fruit on the labels to show their flavour; and electrical machines have red lights to warn people when they're on. Out and about, toilets have symbols of men or women on the doors; road signs have pictures of animals or people digging, while the green man tells us when it is safe to cross the road.

As your child gets older, you can show him that visual signs are often accompanied by

> **'You can use home-made labels as a way of helping your child to recognize new words.'**

words – and some signs are in words only. Many of these are in the street, such as 'Stop!', 'Go', and 'Car Park', while others are on display in restaurants and cinemas, such as 'Way In', 'Exit' and 'Toilets'. You can point out words at home, such as 'tomatoes' on a can, or 'toothpaste' on a tube. Your child won't immediately recognize these words, but they'll soon become familiar.

You can also use home-made labels as a way of helping your child to recognize new words. His name is the most obvious one to start with (see below), but you can also stick labels to items of furniture around the house, such as 'door', 'table', 'chair', 'bed', 'fridge', 'oven' and 'television'. Make sure that all the letters are clear and written in lower case (not capitals) for easy recognition.

play and learn

stuck on you

Buy a sheet of identical stickers (cats or smiley faces, say) and stick them on items belonging to your child: his toybox or coat-peg. As he becomes older, write his name on a blank sticker and stick it next to the original. Take off the original stickers and use only those with his name.

treasure signs

For children just beginning to read, set a mini treasure hunt in which one word card leads to the next – and eventually to a small treat. Good words to try are 'chair', 'table', 'bed', 'bath' and 'toybox'.

favourite things

Make a display of your child's favourite things on a table in his bedroom and write a label for each item. Alternatively, make a display of things that he's collected, such as conkers and acorns.

RESEARCH SAYS

'Syllable and word-shape recognition lead to reading.'

These games help your child to hear the little sounds that make up words and to recognize letters by their shape – both of which are necessary skills for reading. When she can put the two tasks together, she will be ready to spell out letters and blend the sounds to form words.

and today's letter is...

from 4 years

A letter a day is the easy way!

- In the morning, choose a letter together. Say both the name of the letter and the sound it makes clearly for your child.

- During the day, point out lots of different words that begin with that letter, for example, for 'm' you could have Mummy, man, motorbike and milk.

- At the end of the day, ask your child to draw pictures of some of the words to make a letter 'm' poster.

- When she has finished, write the words under the pictures for her and put the poster on the wall.

feely letters
from 5 years

Can your child guess the letter from its shape?

- Choose a letter that your child knows – perhaps the one that begins her name.

- Ask her to face away from you while you draw the letter on her back using your finger. Can she guess which letter you have written?

- If she finds it too difficult, give her a clue, such as 'This letter looks like a wiggly snake'.

- When she is familiar with most letters, you could try spelling out a simple word, such as 'cat' or 'book'. You could also try 'writing' letters on the palm of her hand.

alphabet snap!
from 5 years

Make your own pack of cards to encourage your child to recognize the letters of the alphabet.

- Cut out 52 small cards and divide them into pairs. Working through the alphabet, write a letter and draw a corresponding picture on each pair. For example, the letter 'a' with a picture of an apple; 'b' with a ball; and 'c' with a cat. You'll finish with 26 letter pairs.

- Shuffle the pack of cards, then divide the pack into two. Keep one pile and give the other to your child, face down.

- Take turns to lay down a card. If two are the same, shout, 'Snap!' (allow your child plenty of time) – whoever shouts out first keeps the pair. At the end, count up the pairs and the person with the most pairs is the winner.

- For children who are new to this game, you could use fewer letter pairs and build up to the full alphabet.

count
with me

Gaining confidence with numbers will give your child a great head start when it comes to more formal learning at school. You don't have to be a maths whizz yourself – keep it simple, giving her lots of opportunities to play with numbers, patterns, counting and sorting. This selection of games will help to build her skills in these areas.

RESEARCH SAYS

'Naming numbers is easy, understanding what they mean is much more difficult.'

A number is an abstract concept – you cannot see a 'two', you can only deduce that it represents two dogs, two cars or two bricks. This is why educationalists suggest that the teaching of maths should begin with matching and sorting games, and training children to understand the concept of colour and ownership.

bricks galore
from 2½ years

You can adapt this counting game to match your child's improving number skills.

● Help your child to sort his building bricks into sets of colours.

● Ask if he can build a red tower with two bricks.

● Then ask if he can make a blue tower with three bricks, and so on, depending on how confidently he can count.

● Alternatively, build a little row of towers made with different numbers of bricks, and see if your child can count how many bricks have been used in each tower.

● Finish by taking turns to add a brick to the tallest tower in the world, counting aloud as you go. Whose final brick will send the tower toppling?

colour by numbers
from 4 years

This colour- and number- matching activity is creative as well as educational.

- Draw (or trace) a simple picture such as a fish.

- Divide the picture into clearly marked sections and label them with different numbers. For example, the tail and fins could be number 1, a stripe down the middle number 2, and the remaining sections number 3.

- Draw a colour key on the piece of paper, writing '1' in a red square, '2' in a blue square, and '3' in a green square.

- Ask your child to colour in the fish. Explain that the area marked with '1' should be coloured in red; the number '2' area in blue, and number '3' in green.

guess how many?
from 5 years

Learning to make a sensible estimate is a useful skill that you can help to develop with this easy game.

- Find a clear plastic jar and a mixture of small items to put in it, for example, shells, pebbles and paper clips.

- Show the jar to your child, and ask him to guess how many things there are inside.

- When he has guessed, tip the items out on to a tray and count them together, to see how close his estimate was.

- For an easier game, stick to one type of object, such as shells. For a more challenging game, choose smaller things, such as raisins, or even rice. But be prepared for a long counting session!

33

RESEARCH SAYS

'These games help a child to understand sequential numbers.'

Two is bigger than one and smaller than three. For a child, this is by no means as straightforward as it seems! Try the task with the differently spaced counters (see below right). Research suggests that until children are about five years old, they will say that the longer line has more counters in it. (They will also say that a lump of play dough is bigger when you roll it into a ball than when you squash it flat.)

what's the time, mr wolf?
from 3 years

This counting party game is a favourite with groups of children, but you can play with only two people.

- The 'wolf' turns her back on the other players, who all stand at the other end of the room and call out 'What's the time, Mr Wolf?'

- The wolf turns to face them and says, for example, 'Two o'clock!' The children then take two steps towards the wolf, who then turns away again.

- This is repeated, with the children taking the same number of steps towards the wolf as the 'time' she chooses to give.

- Finally, the wolf responds to the question, 'What's the time, Mr Wolf?' with the answer, 'Dinner time!'

- The wolf then chases the others back to the starting line. Whoever she catches becomes the next wolf.

play-dough numbers
from 3 years

A simple and hands-on way to recognize numbers.

- Roll some pieces of play dough into long, thin sausages.

- Help your child to make numbers from one to ten out of the dough, using different colours.

- If she finds this hard to do 'freehand', draw the numbers on pieces of paper first, and show her how to make the shapes by laying the play dough on top of the numbers.

- When you have finished, your child can trace along each number with her finger to become familiar with its shape.

- She might like to display her numbers on a piece of card so that they show up well.

counting counters
from 4 years

This game helps your child to understand that different shapes can be made with the same objects.

- Show your child six counters (or coins) that are all the same size and colour and ask her to put them in a row.

- Then ask if she can arrange the counters into two rows, with the same number of counters in each row. If this is too easy, how about making three equal rows?

- Explain that she can make a pyramid shape out of these counters, with a row of three, then a row of two, and the last one on top.

- Set out two rows of six counters, with the counters in one row spaced further apart than those in the other. Ask your child which row has the most counters. Can she see that they both have exactly the same number of counters, even though one row is longer than the other?

laying the table

the simplest routines at home can provide a learning opportunity

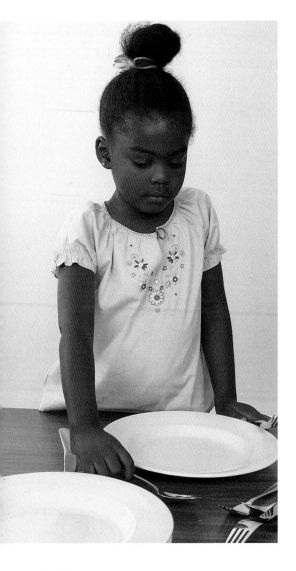

Meal-times are key events in your child's day.

Try to sit down with your child while she's eating, and to have a meal at the same time, if possible, as this helps her understand the social aspect of meals, as well as giving her an example of eating all of the food on her plate. Even if you can't always sit down to eat as a family, you can still make an occasion of meals that you share.

Laying the table is an important part of the process, and something that even a very young child will enjoy helping with. You may find that your child eats better if she feels she has played a part in the preparations for a meal. You will need to take care of your child's safety when handling cutlery – it will make her feel special to have her own child-safe set, and these will have rounded edges and no sharp points.

This is a good opportunity to talk about 'left' and 'right', as you show your child how to put the fork to the left of the plate, and the knife to the right. If you use place mats, she can put these out, too. Discuss whether you

'You may well find that your child eats better if she feels she has played a part in the preparations for a meal.'

will be having pudding, and if you will need to lay out a spoon as well. Let her decide where each place setting should go. For example, if it's just the two of you, would she rather you sit at opposite sides of the table, so that you can chat easily or would she prefer to have you sitting next to her?

Once the places are laid, you can help her to decide what else needs to go on the table.

Will you both want a drink of water? Does the meal need any extras, such as salt and pepper, salad dressing or tomato ketchup? Let your child carry the appropriate items to the table and arrange them where everyone will be able to reach them.

Of course, once the meal is finished, everything needs to be cleared away again, so your child can help you with this too!

play and learn

sorting cutlery

Place all your cutlery – excluding sharp knives – in a jumbled pile on the table. Ask your child to sort the cutlery carefully into knives, forks, tablespoons, and teaspoons. You will need to supervise. Your child will enjoy putting all the cutlery back neatly in the right sections.

come to tea

Invite lots of toys to come to lunch and sit them around a picnic cloth. Set out a selection of real or plastic picnic food. Ask your child to lay a place for each toy using plastic play plates, knives, forks and spoons. Tuck into your picnic lunch together (for real or pretend).

places, please

Cut out strips of paper and fold them in half to form name cards – one for each person (or toy). Help your child to write each guest's name on a card. Let your child decide where everyone will sit and place the cards. Ask your child to call in the rest of the family (or toys) for the meal.

37

getting taller
from 3 years

Children love to have visible evidence that they're growing up, so create a height chart to mark off your child's growth.

● Cut long strips of card or stiff paper and stick them together until you have a piece around 150cm (5ft) long.

● Mark measurements up one side of the height chart – every 10cm (4in) is fine for the first two-thirds; for the final third mark individual centimetres (inches), too.

● Get your child to decorate the chart with pictures of herself as a baby to show how much she has changed!

● Fix the chart to your child's bedroom wall. Every few weeks or months ask her to stand next to it in bare feet. Mark her height on the chart and write the date next to it.

one step, two steps...
from 4 years

Your child can enjoy measuring things indoors or outdoors, simply by using her own two feet!

● Explain that you're going to be doing some measuring today, without using any rulers.

● Ask your child to take the biggest steps she can across the sitting-room, counting them as she goes.

● Then compare the total with the number of steps it takes to get across the kitchen. Measure and compare all the rooms in the house.

● Work out which is the biggest room in the house, and which is the smallest.

● It is also fun to count how many steps it takes to walk to nursery school or the park – if it's not too far!

RESEARCH SAYS

'Abstract ideas are difficult for children to grasp.'

Measuring is one of the easiest ways to show children what numbers mean, because a ruler makes the abstract concept of number concrete – bigger numbers match longer lengths.

as tall as ten
from 5 years

This game helps your child to compare the sizes of familiar objects.

- Find some bricks (or cups) that can be stacked easily.

- Then, find a large toy, such as a teddy bear, and stand it up against a wall for support.

- Stack up the bricks next to the teddy until your tower is the same height as the teddy.

- Together with your child, count how many bricks it takes to be as tall as the teddy.

- Play again with different toys of varying sizes, taking away or adding more bricks as appropriate.

throw to go
from 3 years

Using dice shows your child that numbers form easily recognizable patterns.

- Stand with your child at one end of the sitting-room and take turns to throw a die.

- With each turn, take as many steps as there are dots on the face of the die.

- Gradually work your way across the sitting-room, and see who gets to the other side first.

- With an older child use two dice, which will give basic addition practice as she counts up how many dots there are in total.

chase race
from 3 years

Create your own simple board game to encourage counting skills.

- Find a large sheet of paper, a dark-coloured felt-tip pen, a die and two toy cars (counters or coins will do).

- Ask your child to help you to draw a wide, curvy race-track around the edge of the paper.

- Divide the track down the middle, so that each of you have your own 'road'. Mark the 'start' and 'finish', and draw in numbered squares along each road.

- Take turns to throw the die, count the dots and move along the road accordingly. Whoever reaches the end of the track first is the winner.

RESEARCH SAYS

'Chimps use similar methods for learning numbers!'

Scientists have tried to teach the concept of numbers to chimpanzees – they do learn, but find it extremely difficult. Chimps only succeed when scientists employ methods similar to the ones suggested here. For example, using symbols to create groups (in a pack of cards) and using distance to represent number (in a board game).

card families
from 5 years

There's lots of scope for counting and sorting fun with an ordinary pack of playing cards.

- Show your child how a pack of cards is divided into four suits – hearts, diamonds, spades and clubs.

- Shuffle the pack, then see if she can divide it into a pile of red and a pile of black cards.

- If she can do this with ease, ask her to sort the cards into suits.

- Alternatively, she could put them into number sets, with all the twos together, all the threes together and so on.

- Ask her to make families with the Jack, Queen and King of each suit.

going shopping

*everyday outings are often
the most fun*

An outing to the shops is an opportunity for your child to learn about all sorts of things.

It is always best to choose a time when your child isn't tired or hungry to do the grocery shopping together, as either state will almost inevitably lead to whining and tears in the aisles!

Decide what you're going to buy before setting out. Your child will enjoy helping you to plan what's needed, by talking it through or helping you to write a list.

A supermarket visit offers opportunities to identify and name a wide a variety of foods, especially in the fruit and vegetable section. An older child will enjoy being in

play and learn

my shop

Help your child to set up a little shop of her own by covering a small table with a cloth and letting her set out a selection of items. She can use stickers to label goods with prices. She can be the shopkeeper and you the customer, counting out the money and change as you go.

how heavy?

Put a variety of items on the table. Ask your child to compare two of them, and guess which is heavier. For example, she could compare a tin of beans with a loaf of bread. If she's not sure, she could hold an item in each hand, like a human scale, to help her decide which is heavier.

what goes where?

Ask your child to help you unpack the shopping. As you take the things out of the bags, see if she can sort them into categories. For example, all the fruit; drinks; bread, pasta and rice; all the tins, and so on. Then let her help you to put the groups of items away in the right places.

'An older child will enjoy being in charge of the shopping list and ticking things off as you put them in the trolley.'

charge of the shopping list and ticking things off as you put them in the trolley. You can also talk about which foods need to be protected from getting squashed, such as fruit and vegetables, and which are hard and can be put at the bottom of the trolley, such as cans and packets. Help your child to identify foods that can be eaten together, such as bread and butter, or cereal and milk.

A visit to a smaller shop will involve communication with the shopkeeper, and your child will learn about how important 'please' and 'thank you' are outside the home, too. This is also a good opportunity for your child to observe how different types of money are exchanged, and that you may get coins back as change after paying with a note.

For noise, variety and a general sense of bustling business being done, you can't beat a visit to a market. You can explain that it is generally cheaper to shop in a market because less packaging is generally used and the market is in the open air or a large covered open space.

four seasons collage
from 4 years

A year is a long time in a child's life, and this activity helps him to envisage the changes that take place in that time.

- Find four sheets of paper, some magazines or old catalogues, scissors, and some felt-tip pens or crayons.

- Ask your child to find or draw pictures appropriate to each season of the year, starting with the one you're in. Spring pictures could show baby animals, blossom and spring flowers; for summer, the sun, a beach, a garden in bloom; for autumn, falling leaves, nuts and berries; and for winter, a snowman, gloves, and a log fire.

- Paste them onto the pieces of paper and label each picture with the name of the season.

tick tock clock
from 5 years

Making a pretend clock is a fun way to introduce the concept of telling the time.

- Find a paper plate or cut out a circle of card. You'll also need a brass paper fastener.

- Cut out two hands for the clock, making the minute hand longer than the hour hand. Give each a pointed end, like an arrow.

- Help your child to mark out the numbers on the clock. Use a brighter colour for the 12, 3, 6, and 9.

- Push the paper fastener through both hands of your clock, and fasten them to the centre of the clock face.

- Show him how to set the hands to one o'clock, then ask him to set them to two, three, four o'clock and so on.

- Once he is confident with this, you could try 'half past'.

RESEARCH SAYS

'Learning all about time may take a while and a great deal of practice.'

Our brains contain an inbuilt clock that is set, by the daily pattern of light and dark, to a 24-hour rhythm. But while it may be possible to tell the passing of time and measure intervals using this biological clock, we still have to learn how to read the time, name the seasons and understand the passing of days, weeks and months – all of which take a great deal of practice.

calendar countdown
from 5 years

If your child is looking forward to a special event, such as a birthday party or a trip, this activity will increase his sense of excitement.

- Find a piece of paper and a felt-tip pen. Help your child to draw a row of boxes to represent the number of days left until the big day. Seven to ten days is a reasonable amount for a five-year-old.

- Mark each day with a number from '10' to '1', counting down to the final box, which is the big day.

- For the day, your child could draw a picture to show what it is you're planning to do, such as a birthday cake for a party, a tiger for a trip to the zoo, or a suitcase for going on holiday.

- Your child can tick off each day as it passes, or colour in the box, or stick a coloured star on it. Whichever he chooses, make a little event of it each day.

make a money-box
from 3 years

Children love 'posting' activities, and money is no exception.

- Find a secure container (a small cardboard box or cylinder is ideal) with a removable lid.
- Make a slit in the side of the box – big enough for a coin.
- Ask your child to decorate the box with paint, felt-tip pens, stickers or whatever you have handy.
- Show her how to post and retrieve her coins.
- For an older child, you could seal the money-box with sticky tape until she has saved enough money to buy a particular item. Then open up the box and watch the shower of coins pouring out!

tickets, please
from 3 years

Most children love the adventure of travelling on buses or trains, so take them on a pretend journey in your home.

- Take a piece of paper or card and cut out a selection of rectangles to be the 'tickets'.
- Write the names of places that you and your child would like to visit on each ticket; for example, Grandma's house, the seaside, the toy shop and the swimming pool.
- Find some loose change and take a small pile each. Then take turns to 'sell' each other tickets and enjoy imaginary journeys to the places you've chosen.
- Imagine that the sofa or chair is the bus or the train and hop aboard. As you travel, you can talk to her about what you see, and what you will be able to do when you reach your destination.

money manager
from 4 years

Recognizing the different sets that coins belong to is great early maths practice for your child.

- Find some loose change – check in your pockets, purse and behind the sofa cushions for a good supply.

- Put the coins out in a jumble and ask your child to help you sort them out into piles of identical coins.

- Point out that there are different pictures on either side of the same coin.

- Talk about the different sizes and shapes, and whether the colours are similar or different.

- Make neat towers of the coins and count how many coins there are in each tower.

RESEARCH SAYS

'These games help children to form categories as well as practising numbers and counting.'

Pigeons can differentiate between photographs that have people in them and those that do not. But whether any animals other than humans can form categories by abstracting a common function (for example, that money will buy things) rather than a physical similarity (people present) remains an open question. By the time they are five or six, children can form functional categories. Until then, they use shifting criteria – so, for example, they include items one and two in any given category for entirely different reasons to items five and six.

let's cook

*there's so much your child can learn
with you in the kitchen*

**Cooking is an ever-popular
activity with young children.**

It's a fun way to introduce and practise
lots of different skills, such as weighing,
measuring and timing.

Before starting any kitchen activity, tell your
child how important it is to wash his hands
thoroughly, as germs can't be seen but
could get into the food and make everyone
ill. You may also want to give him a little
apron to wear to help him keep clean.

Talk about which recipe you're going to
follow. A simple cake usually works well.
Even if your child can't read yet, you can
still show him the list of ingredients, and
explain that you'll need him to help you to
find all these things before you start.

As you read out each instruction from the
recipe, ask him to see if he can find the
right ingredients. Let him join in with as
much of the practical action as possible.
He can spoon flour into a bowl or pour
sugar on to the scales. If you allow him to

'Children particularly enjoy mixing, so let him have a large wooden spoon or fork and stir to his heart's content.'

break eggs, make sure he washes his hands again before continuing. Show him how to read the scales, pointing out that the dial reads zero before any food goes into the dish. Children particularly enjoy mixing, so let him have a large wooden spoon or fork and stir away to his heart's content. He'll be able to spoon small amounts of mixture into cake cases but, of course, you'll need to put the tray or cake tin into the hot oven.

If you have a timer, set it together, and check the time on the main clock as well. Talk about how the cakes will be ready when the big hand reaches a particular number. When the cakes are baked and cooled, you can have a tea party together.

play and learn

silly snakes

Help your child roll some pastry into small balls, and then roll out each one into a long thin snake shape. With a fork or cocktail stick, he can prick out markings on his snakes, and stick on currants for eyes. Bake the snakes and, when they have cooled, let him paint them with edible paint.

sandwich shapes

Next time you are making sandwiches, ask your child if he would like them to be triangular or square. Then, ask him how large or small he'd like them to be. Cut them into the right shapes and sizes. If you have little biscuit cutters, he could stamp his sandwiches into fun 'biscuit' shapes.

meals scrap-book

Make a little scrap-book by folding two pieces of paper in half and putting them together. Mark each page 'Breakfast', 'Lunch', 'Tea' and 'Dinner'. Your child can draw pictures of foods that are appropriate for each meal or find pictures from a magazine or catalogue to cut out and stick in.

RESEARCH SAYS

'Children do not rehearse what they need to remember and need our help to do so.'

Skills involving movement and hand-eye co-ordination are best learned by watching a skilled person, trying to remember what they did, then repeatedly practising the activity. Explanation and feedback (praise or simply encouraging him to see for himself that something has worked) are the most important ways a caregiver can help a child to rehearse and remember.

thread it through
from 3 years

Making patterns is easy with this creative threading game.

- Find a selection of pasta shapes that will be easy to thread.

- Divide the pasta into two or three groups, then paint each group a different colour. Leave them to dry thoroughly.

- Show your child how to thread the shapes onto a piece of string or wool.

- Encourage him to form simple patterns with the threading, for example, two red pieces followed by one blue. Then, tie the ends and let him wear the 'necklace'. (Make sure it is long enough for him to remove easily by himself.)

- He could also make pasta patterns by sticking the pieces onto a piece of card.

a stitch in time
from 4 years

Play this game to encourage your child's hand-eye co-ordination, and his shape recognition.

- Cut out some large, basic shapes from a piece of card. Start with a square, a circle and a triangle.

- Make small holes around the inside edge of the shape with a hole-punch or the sharp ends of a pair of scissors.

- Wrap sticky tape securely round the end of a piece of string or wool to make a 'needle'. (A long bootlace is a good alternative.)

- Show your child how to 'sew' by feeding the wool through each hole – counting as you go around the edge of a shape – until he has completed the outline.

copycat squares
from 5 years

This game requires sharp observation skills to match the pattern.

- Draw two identical grids with nine squares in each – three rows and three columns.

- Give one to your child and keep the other. Colour in one of the squares on your grid (make it easy to start with by choosing the central square.)

- Show the grid to your child and ask if he can find the identical square on his own grid to colour in.

- Make the game more difficult for an older child by colouring in more squares in a random pattern for him to copy, or by creating larger grids with more squares.

pencil
and paper

Holding and controlling a pencil
comes naturally to some children,
while others need plenty of practice.
The games here will encourage every child
to enjoy developing good co-ordination,
which will make letter formation and writing
much easier. And a piece of paper is
so much more than just something
to write on – your child can have
great fun cutting, folding
and gluing too.

s-s-stripey snakes
from 3 years

Your child will enjoy bringing basic patterns to life.

- Ask your child to draw a long, wiggly snake.

- Next, draw vertical lines along the length of the snake, dividing it into sections.

- Ask your child to colour each section of the snake in a different colour, being careful to stay inside the lines.

- Finally, your child can give the snake eyes and a long red, forked tongue.

- An older child can draw her own patterns on the snake before colouring them in. Encourage her to create a mixture of shapes, such as zig-zags, spots and stripes.

make a mosaic
from 3 years

This is a craft that has been popular for thousands of years!

- Find several pieces of coloured paper and cut or tear them into small pieces.

- Draw a simple picture outline on a plain piece of paper, for example, a bird, a fish or a cat.

- Ask your child to fill in the outline using the pieces of 'mosaic' paper and a PVA glue stick.

- Finish the picture with a decorative mosaic border.

- An older child will be able to cope with smaller pieces of paper and may be able to create patterns of her own within the mosaic.

RESEARCH SAYS

'Verbalizing cements memory.'

In non-human mammals, the hippocampus (which is situated deep within the brain) is involved in mapping space, keeping track of different views and integrating those views to build up a map of the environment. In humans, the hippocampus also keeps track of verbal memory, and the order and time in which remembered disassociated events happened. Learning how to put things together – and talking about what we do next – practises all these functions.

finish it off
from 4 years

Recognizing patterns is a valuable pre-maths skill.

- Draw a very simple pattern, using two colours, such as a line of alternating red and blue circles.

- Explain how the pattern works, and then ask your child to continue it.

- If she can do this easily, introduce another element, for example, a third colour, or a blue circle followed by a red triangle.

- Continue creating new patterns for your child to follow, then see if she can design one of her own.

55

snowflakes
from 3½ years

Use child-safe scissors for this enduringly popular activity that encourages hand–eye co-ordination.

- Draw round a plate on white paper and cut out the circle.

- Ask your child to fold the paper circle in half, and then in half again, so it forms a triangle shape.

- Using scissors, show him how to snip little sections from along the sides of the triangle, including the curved edge along the bottom.

- When he has finished, he can open out the circle to reveal a beautiful snowflake.

- An older child could colour or paint through the holes on to a fresh piece of paper to create another picture.

plate patterns
from 3½ years

Paper plates are a great resource for practising scissor skills, as they're easy to manipulate yet will also give a satisfyingly sturdy result.

- Give your child a plain white paper plate and a pair of child-safe scissors and ask him to use them to decorate around the outside edge. At first, his snips may be random, but an older child may be able to create a simple pattern all the way around.

- Once he has finished his design, he can colour or paint the rest of the plate.

- You could give an older child a theme for decorating the plate, such as drawing a meal of sausage, chips and peas; a fruit bowl; or perhaps a mini goldfish bowl.

RESEARCH SAYS

'The cerebellum is primarily concerned with the co-ordination of skilled movements.'

The cerebellum – a large, convoluted area at the base of the brain – ensures that skilled movements are smooth and not jerky. It also plays a role in the learning and organization of new skilled movements. Cutting with scissors involves expertise in hand–eye co-ordination and children need practice at this before they finally master cutting complex shapes at around six years old.

maids in a row
from 4 years

Your child can enjoy creating his own imaginary characters with a row of paper figures.

- Find a long rectangular piece of paper and fold it, concertina-style, into six or eight sections.

- Draw a simple figure on the top-most fold. Ensure the 'hands' touch the folded edge of the paper to create a link between the figures.

- Ask your child to cut out the shape with child-safe scissors.

- Then he can unfold the concertina to reveal a row of little figures.

- He can then colour them all in, giving each figure a different face, dress and hair colour. An older child may like to name the figures.

I like lists!

it's never too early to get organized

While some people have sponge-like memories that absorb all the information they need for the day, most of us (and especially children) need reminders about what needs to be done.

Making simple lists is one of the first ways to teach your child how to be methodical.

It also serves as a practical example of using writing in everyday life.

You can point out some of the lists that appear all around us, from the pop charts to your own shopping list for groceries. Talk about how some lists, like the names in a phone book, need to be in alphabetical order. Show her your own address book

play and learn

alphabet shopping

Write the alphabet down the side of a large piece of paper. For each letter, ask your child to think of an everyday shopping item. (For difficult letters, like 'x', choose something with that letter in it!) Your child could search through magazines for pictures to paste on it to bring her list to life.

holiday helper

Plan all the things you'll need to take with you on holiday. If you aren't going on holiday, talk about a picnic or a day out at the seaside. Ask your child to help you make separate lists under headings such as 'Our clothes', 'Things for the beach' and 'Toys and games'.

my busy day

Play this diary-keeping game to exercise your child's memory. Help her make a list of some of the things she did today. Start with 'waking up in the morning', moving on to 'having breakfast', 'going to nursery school', 'having lunch', 'coming home', 'playing', and 'having tea'.

'**Making simple lists is one of the first ways to teach your child how to be methodical.**'

and see how all the names in each section begin with the same letter. Other lists can be in order of preference. For example, when she's thinking of who to invite to her party, the list will probably begin with the people she most wants to have there.

Lists don't have to be written – you can talk to your child about her five favourite items.

But an older child who is starting to write independently may enjoy creating her own personal lists, such as 'My favourite toys', or 'Things I'd like to do tomorrow'. Most children love to mull over what they'd like for their birthday or Christmas, and can keep adding to an ongoing list of suitable presents. For younger children, drawings of each item will work just as well.

copy my boat
from 4 years

Children learn a great deal by imitation, and this game boosts both concentration and observation skills.

- Find two pieces of plain paper and two crayons – one each for you and your child.
- Draw a simple boat on your piece of paper.
- Ask your child to look at it, and then to copy it as carefully as she can onto her own piece of paper.
- Then, your child has a turn, drawing a picture for you to copy.
- A younger child could draw carefully over your picture using tracing paper (or grease-proof paper).

what do you see?
from 5 years

Looking carefully at everyday objects is a simple yet effective way to build observation skills.

- With your child, choose a simple object to draw, such as a piece of fruit, a flower or a leaf.
- Set up your object on the table on a piece of plain paper.
- Ask your child to choose the appropriate coloured crayons and to draw the object as accurately as possible.
- Help your child with tips, such as 'The apple isn't all green is it? Can you see the red part near the stalk? Would you like the red crayon to colour in that part?'.
- When she has finished, display her 'still-life' picture next to the real object, for everyone to admire.

RESEARCH SAYS

'Learning can be "bottom-up" or "top-down".'

The brain makes sense of colour, shape and pattern through both 'bottom-up' processes (building up a complete picture from its component parts – lines, blocks of texture and colour) and 'top-down' processes (the application of organizing principles to what is perceived; getting the overall picture before checking the details). Children learn by practising these processes – slowly building things up a step at a time and/or seeing where they are going first and working out how best to get there later.

brass rubbing
from 4 years

It is fascinating for your child to watch a complex pattern emerging through paper.

- Find an object with a clear pattern or markings on its surface, such as a coin.

- Put a piece of paper on top of the coin.

- Using a soft pencil or wax crayon, show your child how to rub over the coin gently, without letting it slip around under the paper. Be careful to rub over all the outside edges so you get a complete outline.

- Try other items, too, such as dried leaves and shells.

- Your child might enjoy making a display by cutting out each of her brass rubbings and sticking them on to a piece of paper or card.

find the fish
from 3 years

A tracing game that encourages pencil skills.

- Draw three people along one edge of a piece of paper, each holding a fishing rod.

- Next, draw fishing lines for each one, but make them cross over each other so that they are 'tangled'.

- Draw a fish on the end of one of the tangled lines, a boot on the second, and a sock on the third.

- Ask your child to trace along each of the fishing lines, to find out which lucky fisherman has caught the fish.

- Keep the tangles simple for your child's first attempt. If it is too difficult, use a different colour for each line.

my name's dot
from 3½ years

Learning to write her own name is a skill that gives a child great satisfaction.

- Use a pencil to write out your child's name in large letters on a piece of paper.

- Go over the letters with a crayon or felt-tip pen, but use firm dots instead of a continuous line.

- Give your child a crayon and ask her to draw over the dots so that she writes her own name. Encourage her to start from the right place by putting an extra-big dot at the appropriate point on the letter.

- Once she is confident with this, she might be able to try writing her name without the help of the dots.

RESEARCH SAYS

'Develop interconnections between neurones to improve writing skills.'

When a child first learns to write, each stroke of a letter is programmed separately, then each whole letter, gradually building up to the whole word. Eventually, 'networks' of neurones (brain cells) in the child's brain will organize all of the movements needed to write a particular word smoothly and automatically – it is because we have such networks that we find it so difficult to restart our signatures if we stop half-way through.

boxing clever
from 5 years

A challenging, sometimes infuriating, puzzle!

- Draw dots to make a square grid, starting with five rows and five columns.

- Take turns with your child to draw a line joining two of the dots. The object of the game is to create a square by joining four dots – if your line is the one that creates a square, write your initial inside it.

- Once all the dots have been joined, add up how many squares you have each created – whoever has the most is the winner.

- For an older child, increase the size of the grid to make the game more difficult.

keeping charts

*make a record of your child's
interests and achievements*

**A chart is a clear visual way
of reminding your child about
events, or of keeping a record
of her achievements.**

Charts are used all the time in maths, so
by keeping one you'll be encouraging early
maths skills, too.

If you're trying to change a certain type
of behaviour, a chart can be helpful. For
example, if your child keeps getting up in
the night to come into your bed, keeping
you awake, you could make a chart that
records how many nights she hasn't
disturbed you. This will be a good incentive
for her to stay in her own bed. Involve your
child in creating the chart and in filling in
the results, making a little ceremony of this
each day.

If your child is working towards a particular
goal, it is also helpful to have a reward. Let
her know there will be a little treat once her
chart has been completed. As waiting is
difficult for little children, keep this to just a
few days at a time.

> **'If you're trying to change a certain type of behaviour, a chart can be most helpful.'**

You could make a bar chart that records how many times your child does something good during the week. For example, she can draw an apple, an orange, a banana and grapes along the bottom of the chart and colour in the appropriate square each day, depending on which fruit she has eaten. She will enjoy seeing her chart grow a little every day.

Another practical chart is one which shows what activities your child has planned for each day of the week. To make your chart, divide a piece of paper into seven vertical columns, write the day of the week at the top of each column and then add in the activities you do on each day, such as going to playgroup or gym class, visiting Grandma and going to a birthday party.

play and learn

you're a star

Mark out a chart with the days of the week down one side. Every day, when your child successfully completes a given target – such as finishing her dinner – she can add a star to the chart. Stick-on stars are always popular, but you could draw the star and ask your child to colour it in.

winner's certificate

If your child has done something special, she'll enjoy being praised for her success. Create a certificate that she can display proudly in her room. You can do the writing, while your child decorates the certificate with a border, stickers or pictures.

growing up

Make a picture chart that follows the progress of several living things, so that your child can see how they grow. You could start with a seed that sprouts a root and shoot, then leaves and finally becomes a flourishing plant with flowers.

swirly whirlies
from 3 years

Encourage careful colouring with this simple game that starts with lots of scribbles.

- Give your child a crayon or pencil and ask him to do some scribbling on a piece of paper.

- When he has finished, point out that the scribbles have created lots of funny shapes where the lines cross over.

- Ask him to colour in each of the shapes in a different colour, being careful not to go over the lines.

- He may want to finish by outlining all of the shapes in a felt-tip pen.

- An older child will enjoy the challenge of ensuring that no two adjoining shapes are the same colour.

four little cats
from 3 years

Your child can create unique 'pets' with this colouring activity.

- Draw outlines of four identical cat shapes.

- Talk about the cats with your child, and ask him what he thinks they might look like.

- Choose appropriate coloured crayons or felt-tip pens and ask your child to give each cat a different look. The first could be black and white, the second ginger, the third completely black and the fourth a tabby.

- Add simple features to the first cat, such as eyes, a nose, a mouth and whiskers. Your child can repeat the process for cats two, three and four.

- Finally, ask your child to give each cat a name and decide which one he would like best as a pet.

RESEARCH SAYS

'When colouring up to the edge of a drawing, a child uses careful hand–eye co-ordination.'

Scientists have shown that this careful 'checked out' movement is controlled by the cerebral cortex of the brain – the part that is just under the skull. Filling in the rest of the colour is best done with a flowing hand and flowing movement is controlled by the cerebellum, which is at the base of the brain.

paper pizza
from 3 years

By folding a circle of paper, your child can discover the fun of creating patterns, and there are lots of opportunities for imaginative variations.

- Cut out a large circle of paper – you could draw round a dinner plate.

- Ask your child to fold the paper circle in half, then in half again, and in half for a third time.

- Ask him to unfold it, revealing that the circle is now divided neatly into eight portions.

- Your child can then colour each section carefully with a different-coloured crayon or felt-tip pen to create a dazzling colour circle.

- You could suggest making the circle into a pizza that's been sliced into eight, and draw different tasty toppings for each section.

RESEARCH SAYS

'At first, children scribble, then they see possibilities in their scribbles.'

Most psychologists who have studied children's drawings believe that the step from scribble to figurative drawing probably happens rather like these games. Children first draw or paint at random, then look at what they have done and see, in the loop of a scribble or a blob of paint, the possibility of making a face, so they add the eyes. Because it delights them – and it delights us – they do it again.

crazy prints
from 3 years

The joy of giving is extra exciting for your child when the gift is wrapped in her own hand-printed paper.

- Slice a large potato in half lengthways.

- Carve a simple shape into one half – for example, the first letter of your child's name, a heart or a star – creating a potato stamp.

- Let your child dip the stamp into some poster paint, then print it on to some plain wrapping paper, repeating until the paper is well decorated.

- Once it is dry, your child can wrap a present, or simply display the paper as a work of art.

- An older child might also like to print a matching card and gift tag.

going blobby
from 3½ years

From a simple blob of ink or paint, it's amazing where your child's imagination can lead.

- Let your child blob a little ink or paint from a brush on to a piece of paper. Make sure he is wearing an apron to protect his clothes before he starts.

- Fold the piece of paper in half, then open it out to see what interesting shape the blob has made.

- Let it dry, then ask your child to add his own drawings to the blob to create a completely new picture. For example, he might add legs to make a spider; a head and legs to make a person; or wings to create a butterfly.

wacky pictures
from 5 years

Encourage your child to explore possibilities with this drawing game.

- Do a random scribble on a piece of paper.

- Show it to your child and ask if he can create a real picture from the scribbled outline.

- If he finds this difficult, make some suggestions. For example, 'How about putting two eyes here, and two big ears – then it'll look just like a mouse.'

- Then, let him do a scribble and you can have a turn at making a picture out of it.

writing greeting cards

making and decorating cards and letters are practical pre-writing skills

Well before your child can read and write letters and cards, she will understand the excitement of opening envelopes to reveal colourful pictures.

Birthdays, in particular, are exciting events at which cards mean a great deal. Creating cards for special occasions is an activity that most children enjoy. It is also a great pre-writing skill, as it shows your child how easy – and how much fun – it is to communicate good wishes on paper.

Even when there isn't any particular event to celebrate, encourage your child to draw a special picture on a piece of folded paper and 'write' a message inside that she can

play and learn

name cards

Fold a piece of paper in half and carefully mark out the initial (or age) of the person you're sending it to. With child-safe scissors, your child can cut around most of the outline of the letter or number so that forms the front of the card, then he can decorate it.

first writing

If your child is starting to practise letters, encourage him to write a message inside the card. Write or dot-to-dot the words very faintly in pencil first, then ask your child to write over your marks.

wish you were here

Help your child to make pretend postcards to send to friends and family (if you don't have any spare postcards, he could always make some of his own). Ask him to dictate a message for you to write on the back and then let him add a funny stamp as a finishing touch!

'Encourage your child
to create her own cards for all
the major festivals that you
celebrate in your family.'

give to someone in the family. This is a particularly nice way to keep in touch with relatives who live at a distance.

As your child's writing skills progress, she can start to put her name on the card, and add some 'x's for kisses at the bottom. If you write out a short message, such as, 'I miss you', your child might be able to copy or trace the letters herself.

Encourage your child to create her own cards for all the major festivals that you celebrate in your family. Most people get far more enjoyment from receiving a home-made card from a child than a shop-bought one. Always use stiff card and stock up on some large envelopes. A supply of felt-tip pens, crayons, stickers, glitter and stars will also be useful for enhancing decoration still further.

funny faces
from 4 years

Understanding other people's facial expressions is an important skill, which this game helps your child to exercise.

- Draw four circles, giving each one hair but no features.

- Add eyes, nose and a smiley mouth to the first face, and ask your child if that person is happy or sad.

- For the second face, draw a sad, down-turned mouth and ask your child to guess how that person is feeling.

- Next, do a cross face (eyebrows pointing down in the middle) and a surprised one (eyes and mouth wide open).

- Let your child draw some faces and expressions so that you can guess which is which. Then, have fun making the faces yourselves!

animal magic
from 4 years

Children love to feel they're clever and know the answer, and this game encourages that sense of achievement.

- Draw the outline of an animal, such as a pig, a horse, a chicken or a cow. Leave out its main identifying features, so that your child can draw them in.

- Ask your child to add the appropriate tail, such as a curly one for a pig or a long, flowing one for a horse.

- Next, ask her to try adding the right number of legs – four for a pig, two for a chicken!

- Continue with any other important features, for example, eyes, a nose and a mouth.

- Finally, ask your child if she can make the right noise for the animal she has created.

RESEARCH SAYS

'Research shows that when children first add details to their drawings, they rarely count!'

In children's drawings, the animals may have more than four legs and the people may have more (or fewer) than five fingers. These games encourage children to think more about the detail in their drawings as well as improving their general observational skills.

mirror matching
from 5 years

This kind of matching requires lots of careful observation and pencil control.

- Fold a piece of paper in half, and open it out again.

- On one side of the fold, draw one half of a shape, such as a circle.

- Ask your child to complete the shape by drawing a mirror-image copy on the other side of the fold.

- Once she has mastered this, move on to slightly more complex shapes, such as a star, a diamond or an irregular wiggly pattern.

- She may then be able to complete a picture of half a person, an animal or a house.

- She can enjoy colouring in the finished pictures.

73

hitting the right note

Music can bring a new dimension
to learning – whether children are
listening to it or making it themselves.
These games use music in a variety
of ways, encouraging children to stretch
their imaginations, recognize rhythm
and dance to the beat. There's
no end to the pleasure that
music can bring!

one, two, three
from 2½ years

Dance helps your child to recognize rhythm and practise co-ordination.

- Choose a piece of music with a swinging rhythm – such as a three-beat waltz.
- Carry your child in your arms or let him stand on your feet as you hold each other.
- Move to the music, counting out the time as you go.
- See if your child can count out the beat himself.
- With an older child, pretend you're at a dance, and talk about what you're wearing, and how many players there are in the orchestra or band.

mirror dance
from 4 years

This is a simple copy-cat game that stretches your child's observational skills.

- Choose some up-beat music that you and your child enjoy dancing to.
- Ask your child to pretend there's a mirror between you, and that he is your reflection.
- As you move, your child should simultaneously imitate your movement as precisely as possible. (Keep your dance slow and controlled to begin with, to make it easier for him.)
- When he is more confident, try variations, such as jerky robotic movements, smooth ballerina poses, or lively disco moves.

RESEARCH SAYS

'Brain cells called "mirror" neurones become excited when face-to-face with someone performing the same action.'

The fact that these neurones recognize the mirror image means the networks feeding them must be able to 'flip' the image – turn the 'left' movements we see into 'right' ones. Some scientists believe this ability to take a whole image and look at it from another angle underlies our ability to view ourselves from the outside and mimic what others do.

the grand party
from 4 years

A great opportunity to dress up and feel special!

- Pretend that you and your child are guests at an extremely grand ball.

- Put on some classical music and invite your child to dance, bowing or curtseying low as you do so.

- Encourage him to bow or curtsey in return, before joining you on the 'dance floor'.

- Try doing a formal dance together in which you step elegantly across the room holding hands, bow or curtsey at the end of the room, before stepping back across to finish the dance.

- Girls might enjoy wearing long dresses, or just tucking a trailing piece of fabric into their waist bands, while boys can wear bow ties and sashes (real or paper).

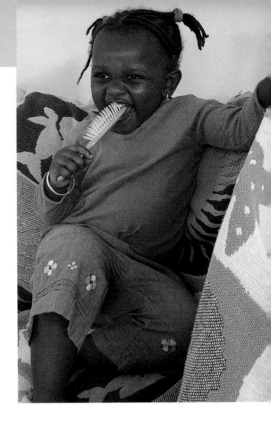

RESEARCH SAYS

'Many scientists believe there is a connection between mathematical and musical skills.'

It is certainly the case that many skilled mathematicians are good musicians – and vice versa. Language is predominantly controlled by the left-hand side of the brain, music, maths and spatial understanding are predominantly controlled by the right-hand side. For this reason, by exercising your child's ear for music, you could also be improving her mathematical prowess.

piano forte
from 3 years

Get ready to make some big sounds!

- Talk about how different things sound when you say them quietly, and when you say them loudly. For example, people may sound excited when they talk loudly, or shy when they whisper.

- Explain that 'piano' is a musical word for 'quietly', while 'forte' means 'loudly'.

- Ask your child to sing a familiar song 'piano', then to sing it 'forte'.

- Of the songs she knows, which does she think sound best sung quietly or loudly?

- An older child may be able to swap half-way through a song when you call out a new instruction.

fast-forward
from 4 years

This game helps your child to understand the importance of tempo (speed).

- Pretend that you and your child are performers on a CD, singing a favourite nursery rhyme or song together.
- Press the imaginary fast-forward button – the CD player speeds up and you have to sing as quickly as possible.
- Take your finger off the button for normal play.
- Then speed up again and sing fast once more.
- You could dance, too, so that when you are singing fast, you look like a music video on fast-forward.

see-saw scales
from 5 years

Teach your child to recognize and sing musical scales.

- Start by singing a low note, then continue singing a musical scale going up.
- Ask your child if the see-saw scale is on its way up, or down.
- Next, try starting on a high note and singing a scale coming down. Can she identify this as up or down?
- To vary the game, sing two notes, and ask your child which is higher and which is lower.
- Ask her to sing two notes, or scales, so that you can have a turn at identifying them.
- An older child may enjoy identifying high and low notes within favourite songs.

enjoying music

*discover the pleasure
of sharing music*

Young children love music and respond positively to it – attend any open-air music concert and you'll usually see a group of toddlers dancing near the stage!

Music can help to create a particular mood – put on a busy pop song if you want to dance and jump around; some gentle ballet music for quiet concentration; or a relaxing piano piece if you want to calm things down at the end of the day.

As well as using music to accompany activities, spend some time listening to music and focusing on it completely. Introduce your child to different sorts of music, such as instrumental, vocal, jazz, blues, classical, ballet and folk. Listen in short stretches and if your child becomes

play and learn

musical shapes

Put on some music that has loud and quiet sections and ask your child to dance to it, making herself into a big shape for the loud sounds and a small shape for the quiet ones.

orchestra conductor

Using a pencil for a baton, your child can beat time by moving her arm up, down and to the side in a rough right angle. When the music gets louder, she can wave her arms in the air; and when it gets quieter, she can put her finger to her mouth.

air instruments

Everyone loves playing air guitar, so why not mime playing other instruments, too? Good ones for your child to try include the trumpet, piano, triangle, trombone and drum.

'Introduce your child
to different sorts of music, such as
instrumental, vocal, jazz, blues,
classical, ballet and folk.'

fidgety encourage her to close her eyes, or try lying on the sofa with her head in your lap while you stroke her hair.

If your child needs something specific to focus on, suggest she listens out for a particular instrument, such as a flute, piano or drums, and waves her hand in the air when she hears it. Or ask if she can spot when the music is getting faster or slower (tempo), or louder or quieter (dynamics). You could also ask her how the music makes her feel, and what sort of things it makes her think of.

Taking your child to a concert can make for an exciting day out. The best ones for young children are free events held in open spaces, indoors or outside, where your child has plenty of room to move around and you can leave whenever her interest flags. Look out for preschool music classes in your area, too. These are usually great fun for all and enable your child to participate in singing and dancing with other children, as well as trying out some musical instruments, such as shakers, triangles and bells.

fairies and giants
from 3 years

Discover how sound can spark your child's imagination.

- Pretend to be big, angry giants stomping around.

- Next, tip-toe, pretending to be the fairies who live in the giant's house. Explain you're so light and delicate that you scarcely make a sound as you flit to and fro.

- Make up a story together about what happens in the giant's house and what other noises there might be: creaking doors, mice scratching under the floor, a baby crying and the fairies' wands crackling with magic.

- Try to represent the characters with high and low notes, played loudly or quietly on a piano or keyboard.

animal songs
from 3 years

The amazing range of sounds in the natural world can introduce your child to the concept of pitch.

- Talk about how animals make different noises.

- Ask your child if she can think of some creatures that make high-pitched noises, such as a squeaking mouse, a trilling bird and a bat whose cry is so high-pitched that we can't even hear it.

- Then, ask your child to identify animals that make low-pitched sounds, such as a growling bear, a trumpeting elephant and a mooing cow.

- Have fun making the noises – your child might enjoy acting out the animals' behaviour, too.

- See if your child can sing a favourite nursery rhyme using animal sounds.

RESEARCH SAYS

'Memory can be "implicit" or "explicit".'

With few exceptions, it is impossible to recall exactly what something looks, feels, sounds or smells like, or how we perform a skilled movement. Such memories are implicit – we need strong cues in order to remember them. On the other hand, music and language are explicit – we can immediately 'summon up' a tune or the story of what we did in words. These games take sounds and ask children to remember them explicitly, or at will, by forming associations between the sounds and stories.

musical stories
from 4 years

Add some music and sound effects to a favourite story.

- Tell your child that you're going to tell her a favourite story, but you want her to provide the soundtrack.

- For *Goldilocks and The Three Bears*, for example, she will need to make the sounds of a creaky door, the crash of a broken chair, and the clinking of a spoon as Goldilocks eats the porridge. For *The Three Little Pigs*, she could use some scratchy straw, crackling twigs and two stones to tap together for bricks.

- An older child could make up scary, exciting or soothing tunes to go with characters such as Goldilocks or the Big Bad Wolf.

what am I playing?
from 4 years

This game draws your child's attention to how musical instruments are played.

- Pretend that you and your child are in a band or orchestra and there are lots of instruments around.

- Pick up an imaginary instrument and start to 'play' it. Ask your child if he can guess which instrument you are playing.

- If he finds it difficult, you could help him by making the sound of the instrument, or giving a clue, such as, 'You have to bang it with sticks to make the noise'.

- Good instruments to mime include drums, a triangle, a piano, a trumpet, a guitar and a recorder.

- Let your child have a turn to play, and you do the guessing.

hot and cold music
from 4 years

In this treasure hunt, the clues your child follows are sounds.

- Hide a little prize, such as a toy or a book, somewhere in the house or garden.

- Start the game well away from the prize, and ask your child to hunt for it.

- Help him by singing or humming quietly when he is nowhere near the prize and increasing the volume of your singing the closer he gets to it.

- You could use a CD or radio, turning the volume up and down, but this means you'll need to keep the hunt to just one room.

RESEARCH SAYS

'Music skills, like language skills, rely on listening and the careful observation of detail.'

Just like the little sounds that make up words, the individual sounds that make up a tune 'matter', and just as children need practice with language, they need practice with musical sounds.

name that tune
from 5 years

Challenge listening skills and build a song.

- Tell your child that you're going to think of a tune that he knows well.

- Sing the first word and ask if he can guess what the tune is.

- It's unlikely he'll get it in one, so sing again, this time with two words.

- Continue, adding a word each time, until he recognizes the song.

- Praise him for guessing so quickly, then sing the whole song together.

- An older child will enjoy challenging you to name his tune, too.

making instruments

*use everyday household goods
to make musical instruments*

Making musical instruments your child can play is a great craft activity, and playing with them afterwards is lots of fun.

The most obvious instrument to start with is a shaker made from dried lentils in a plastic bottle – make sure the top is securely sealed before your child starts to shake it! Different sounds can be made with different shaker combinations, so experiment with various types of dried foods, such as peas, rice or beans, and different-sized plastic bottles and pots.

You could make a drum by stretching a balloon over a bowl and securing it with sticky tape, or by putting grease-proof paper over a tin and securing it with a couple of elastic bands; a tambourine by attaching foil circles to the edge of a paper plate; and a guitar by stretching elastic bands vertically around an empty tissue box and adding a ruler for a fingerboard. Blowing through a piece of paper wrapped around a comb, or banging two halves of a coconut together will also make interesting

'**Even two saucepan lids banged together can become cymbals.**'

sounds. Even two saucepan lids banged together can become a pair of cymbals.

You can find packs of little bells in many craft shops. Thread these on to string or ribbons – remember to tie knots between the bells to stop them sliding together – to make jingly bangles to tie around your child's wrists and ankles.

One experiment that's fun to try – with careful supervision – is lining up a row of jam jars and filling them with increasing amounts of water. When your child taps each one it will produce a slightly different note, enabling her to play a simple tune on them. Alternatively, fill plastic bottles with varying amounts of water. Your child can blow across the top to make different notes.

play and learn

play along

Put on a CD and ask your child to play along with her home-made instruments. Ask her to match her instrument to the one she can hear on the CD – changing over from drum to guitar, for example, as the music changes.

which instrument?

If you have a tape recorder, make a recording of each home-made instrument in turn, then play the tape back to see if your child can guess which instrument each sound has come from.

form a band

Invite some other children to your house and give each one a home-made instrument. Make a band and have a music parade around the garden. Ask everyone to play as loudly as they can!

pop stars
from 4 years

Bring out the performer in your child!

- Lay out some cushions in your sitting room so that they look like a stage.

- Find a wooden spoon to use as a microphone.

- Pretend you are announcing a brand new up-and-coming star and would like to welcome... (your child's name)... to the stage.

- Hand your child the microphone and let her sing you her favourite song or rhyme.

- Give her a big round of applause when she has finished!

musical echoes
from 5 years

Copying a melody helps your child to think about individual notes.

- Tell your child you are going to sing something to her and that you would like her to pretend to be an echo in a cave and sing it back to you.

- Start with a short tune she already knows and sing it clearly, but using 'la la' sounds instead of the words.

- If she manages to sing it correctly, try making up a tune and see if she can also echo this. Use only a few notes to begin with (four is probably enough), and then build up to a longer tune.

- Can you echo some of her tunes?

RESEARCH SAYS

'Social games stretch children further than games played with objects.'

Research suggests that whenever a small child learns something new about the world around her – for example, that things continue to exist even when she can no longer see them – she first does so in a social context. For a small child, music is a social activity, and even if she never joins a choir, these basic musical skills open the door to shared musical experiences.

round and round we go!

from 5 years

Singing in a round is difficult but fun – it is an ideal game to play in the car.

● Explain to your child that a round is where everyone sings the same song, but starts at different times.

● Start with a song that she knows well, for example, *London's Burning* or *Kookaburra*. Ask her to sing it and tell her that you'll join in when she's on the second line. Sing softly so that you don't put her off!

● Stick to two parts to begin with, but gradually build up to more parts as she gets better.

● As your child's confidence increases, you can play the game with more people and more singing parts.

mini metronomes
from 2½ years

Can your child clap to the beat of his favourite song?

- Choose a nursery rhyme or song that has a strong, even beat. For example, *Twinkle, Twinkle, Little Star* or *Little Bo Peep*.
- Sing the song slowly with your child, clapping out the beat as you sing it.
- Encourage your child to clap in time with you. Don't worry if he doesn't get it right first time as this is quite a challenge to begin with.
- Instead of clapping a basic beat, older children could try clapping to each note of a more complicated song.

clap your name
from 3 years

Use names to make a game and introduce the concept of syllables.

- Count how many syllables there are in your child's name. For example, 'Ben' is one syllable, 'Ho-lly' is two syllables and 'Nich-o-las' is three syllables.
- Show your child how to say his name slowly and clap on each syllable.
- When he has managed this, see if he can add his surname. For example, 'Nich-o-las John-son'.
- Clap out other names within the family. Whose name has the most syllables? Whose has the least? Are there any other words he could clap out in this way?

RESEARCH SAYS

'Refined movement comes from the cerebellum.'

Movement is initiated by the frontal cortex of the brain, but the control of smooth movements takes place in the cerebellum. When a child is working out when to clap, the movements are probably controlled by the frontal cortex; once he is skilled at clapping, however, the cerebellum has taken over.

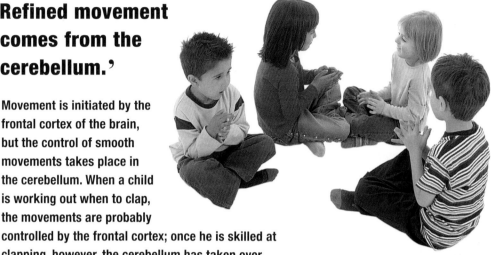

two can play
from 4 years

Interactive hand-clapping games are a playground favourite, so give your child a head-start.

- Sit opposite your child and tell him you're going to play a game in which you clap hands at the same time.

- Start with a very simple routine in which you both clap your own hands together once and then clap one hand on each of your thighs.

- When he has got the hang of this, add to the routine, so that you both clap your own hands again and then each other's (palms together).

- See if you can start slowly and gradually speed up – or sing a song while you play.

- For an older child, build up the routine, adding extra claps, such as opposite hands or knees.

identifying sounds

careful listening is a vital early-years' skill for your child

One of the best ways to encourage your child to listen well is to help her to identify sounds and distinguish their meanings and patterns.

The most obvious sound of all is speech. Being a good listener will not only help your child to make friends, but it is also essential when she's being given instructions by a teacher at nursery school. She'll expand her vocabulary as she listens to different patterns of speech around her, and improve her concentration skills, too.

Make time to have proper conversations together, so that she understands that you each take turns to speak and respond. Try to be on her eye-level as you chat, and let her know that her thoughts and opinions are interesting and valued.

Encourage her to listen to sounds outside – some sounds you may hear, for example, are birdsong, children playing, lawnmowers buzzing, and the wind rustling leaves. Take it in turn to name the sounds you can both hear.

'**Your child might enjoy drawing pictures to represent all the sounds she has heard – inside and out.**'

On a trip into town you could talk about the sounds that have an important meaning which everyone understands, for example, a police car siren, the beeping of a road crossing, the chiming of a town clock, or the enticing tune of an ice cream van!

There's plenty to hear inside the house, too, if you listen carefully. See if you can count ten sounds together, such as the humming of the heating system, a dripping tap, the clock ticking, and a car passing by outside the window.

Your child might enjoy drawing pictures to represent all the sounds she has heard – both inside and out.

play and learn

hidden sounds	travel sounds	where's the sound?
Take a selection of items that make a sound and hide them behind a screen or the sofa. Then, make the sounds and ask your child if she can guess what they are. Try crackling a newspaper, tapping a jar with a spoon, flicking through a book or squeaking a toy.	When you're out and about in the car, bus or train, ask your child to identify as many different sounds as she can. For example, in the car she might hear the car engine, the clicking of the indicators, the heater blowing air, voices, the radio and other car horns.	Ask your child to sit in the centre of the room with her eyes closed. Creep to another part of the room and make a very quiet sound – maybe an animal noise, or saying her name. Your child has to point to where she thinks the sound was coming from. Then, ask her to open her eyes to see how close she was.

marching parade
from 2 years

Get ready to march in time to the beat!

- Put on some rhythmic, up-beat music or you can simply sing a lively nursery rhyme, such as *The Grand Old Duke Of York*.

- Choose some pretend marching instruments, such as a drum, trumpet or big cymbals.

- With you leading the way, march together around your sitting-room (or even the house) in time to the beat.

- Make the game more fun by occasionally shouting 'Turrrn right!', 'Turrrn left!', and 'Halt!'. Always show your child which direction you mean.

pat the rhythm
from 4 years

Can your child remember a rhythm and pat it back?

- Explain to your child that musical notes can be different lengths and that's what gives a tune its rhythm.

- Tell him you're going to pat a rhythm on your legs and ask him if he can copy it on his legs.

- Pat out a very simple rhythm at first, such as, 'long, short, short, long', or, 'long, long, short, short, long'.

- Try some other rhythms, but remember to keep them very simple and short.

RESEARCH SAYS

'Music stimulates the brain's pleasure and reward centre.'

If the area of the brain associated with pleasure and reward (the limbic system, situated under the cerebral cortex) is over-stimulated, animals make rhythmical movements, such as shaking their heads and running around in circles. Listening to and making music are examples of a large number of rhythmical activities we find enjoyable; dancing and running are other obvious contenders.

what's my song?
from 5 years

Tap out a rhythm on your child's back and see if he can identify which song it is.

- Think of a favourite song such as 'Happy Birthday' or 'Jingle Bells', and tap it out gently on your child's back.

- Ask if he can guess the song you tapped.

- If it is too difficult, give him some clues, such as 'This is one we sing at night-time', or 'This one is about a cow who jumped over the moon'.

- Tap it out again once he's got the correct answer.

can you remember?

A good memory is a great asset that's invaluable throughout life. You can help to develop and stimulate your child's memory skills with these simple games – from recalling a story he has heard to playing a visual card game.

what did we see?
from 2½ years

Use a favourite television programme to stretch your child's short-term memory.

● Watch one of your child's favourite television programmes with her.

● When it has finished, switch off the TV and tell your child you're going to play a game to see how much she can remember.

● Start with simple questions, such as the names of the main characters and build up to more difficult questions about what happened in today's programme.

● Pretend to remember something yourself, but get it slightly wrong so that your child can correct you.

copy me
from 3 years

Can your child copy a sequence of actions?

● Tell your child that you're going to perform an action and you want her to copy you. You could try touching your toes, putting your hands on hips or patting your leg.

● If she can manage this, give her two actions to copy in succession, such as touching her toes followed by patting her leg.

● See if she can build up to copying three, or even four, actions in a row.

● Then, make the game more difficult by describing the actions instead of demonstrating them.

best birthday!
from 4 years

Cast your child's mind back to a special day.

- Start by saying 'Do you remember when it was your birthday and we had a big cake?'.

- If your child says yes, ask her if she can remember what the cake looked like. Can she remember cutting it? Was it at her party? Did she and her friends play games together? What were those games?

- Carry on asking questions until you have reminisced about all the nice things that marked that day, such as the presents, the cards and the decorations.

RESEARCH SAYS

'Small children need help to make memory explicit.'

When adults need to remember something, they automatically rehearse and link events and instances to help them recall the to-be-remembered thing. To do this, they translate the experience into words, making memory explicit. Small children do not automatically make memory explicit, so they will need help from you to enable them to recall things.

99

hunt the ball
from 2 years

Your child has to notice the 'hidden' object in familiar surroundings.

- Show your child a small ball and tell him you're going to hide it. Ask him to close his eyes for a few seconds.

- Place the ball somewhere in the room, at child-height and uncovered, for example, next to the sofa leg or on a shelf with several other items.

- Tell your child to open his eyes and look around to see if he can find the ball.

- You could speed up the game by seeing if your child can find the ball before you've finished counting down from 20 or 10.

teddy's scarf
from 4 years

Can your child remember a pattern and reproduce it?

- Draw a teddy and give him a scarf divided into three sections. Colour each section a different colour.

- Show the picture to your child and ask him to remember the colours on Teddy's scarf. When he has had a good look, turn the picture over.

- On another piece of paper, draw a similar teddy and ask your child to colour in the scarf the same way you did.

- When he has finished, turn over the original drawing to see if it matches.

- For an older child, add extra details, such as a spotted bow-tie, stripy shorts or a T-shirt with a star on it.

RESEARCH SAYS

'Small children are not usually aware that they know something until they return to the situation.'

Your child may only remember feeding the ducks as hazy images until he is reminded by seeing the ducks again. Encouraging children to tell the story of their experiences (or telling them the story) helps them to lay down an explicit memory of events making it possible for them to recall what happened at will. Try to reinforce all of these activities with the spoken word.

kim's game
from 4 years

Adults and children can test their memories with this favourite party game.

- Put a selection of ten small objects on a tray and make a list of them. The selection could include items such as comb, a set of keys, a die, a toy soldier, a fork, an apple and a pen, for example.

- Ask your child to look at the objects and try to remember them all.

- After a minute or two, take the tray away and ask your child to name as many objects as he can, while you tick them off the list. How many can he remember?

- For an older child, increase the number of objects on the tray.

remembering what you've don

*recalling events helps to clarify
them in your child's mind*

Make sure all the family is settled at the dinner table, then open the conversation by recalling something you and your child experienced together that day. For example, you could say, 'Outside nursery school, we saw a naughty baby pull off her sock, didn't we, Kate?'

Then, encourage your child to add her memories, by gently asking her questions starting with 'who', 'what', 'where', 'how' and, 'why'. When you have talked about things you've done together, move on to an experience you didn't share. Describe to her something nice, funny or unusual that happened to you. Then, ask her to tell you about something that happened to her while you weren't there, perhaps at nursery school. Listen to what she says and try to expand her story by asking a few leading questions.

Young children live very much in the present, so recalling what happened yesterday can be quite a challenge. It's a

'Young children live very much in the present, so recalling what happened yesterday can be quite a challenge.'

useful thing to do, however, as it helps her to understand the idea of 'today', 'yesterday' and 'tomorrow'. Give her some clues to help her, such as 'We went to Aunty Sue's yesterday, didn't we? Do you remember what game we played while we were there?'. When your child is confident about remembering yesterday, you can move on to things that happened last week or last month, though you may need something visual, such as a photograph or a leaflet, to prompt her memory.

A special event, such as a visit to the circus or a day by the sea is something exciting to remember. Keep a few mementoes to remind you of the event, such as the programme, or a collection of sea shells.

play and learn

tell the puppet

Put on a glove puppet and use it to talk to your child. Pretend the puppet knows nothing about zoos or farms and needs your child to tell him all about them.

regular events

Activities that happen each week are useful 'pegs' for your child's memory. Try putting out clues to help her guess what you're going to do that day, such as leaving her swimming costume and towel at the bottom of the stairs.

imagine tomorrow

When you put your child to bed, talk to her about all the nice things she will be doing tomorrow and encourage her to imagine what they might be like. Hopefully, she'll wake up the next morning full of happy anticipation.

who am I thinking of?

from 2 years

Can your child recognize a character from a nursery rhyme?

- Tell your child that you want her to guess who you're thinking of, and that you are going to give her a clue.

- Choose a nursery rhyme that your child knows well, such as *Jack And Jill* and select part of it as your clue. For example, 'The people I am thinking of went up a hill to "fetch a pail of water"'.

- If your child finds this easy, try saying a line from a rhyme and asking for its title, for example, 'Which rhyme includes the line, "the cow jumped over the moon"?'.

- You could play with famous fairytale characters, too.

tell me the story

from 3½ years

Read a story, then ask your child to retell it.

- Read your child a well-known story, such as *Little Red Riding Hood*.

- When you have finished, close the book and ask your child if she can remind you of the story.

- If she has trouble starting, give her a clue by saying, 'Let's see, the little girl had to go and visit her grandmother, didn't she. Now, who did she meet in the forest on the way?'

- If she gets stuck half-way, go back and look at the pictures in the book to remind her what happened next.

what was it like?
from 5 years

Help your child to visualize and reconstruct a scene.

- Let your child choose a theme, such as the seaside, a busy street, the park, or a funfair.

- Tell her that you're going to describe a scene on that theme and ask her five questions about it afterwards. She will get a point for every correct answer.

- When you have finished, start asking questions, such as 'Were the ducks on the pond white or brown?', and 'Was there a see-saw in the playground?'.

- For older children, make the description more complicated, and ask more questions.

RESEARCH SAYS

'These activities exercise your child's auditory memory – to put words to pictures.'

Psychologists who have studied how young children learn find that they do not automatically rehearse what has happened to them, which means that they are much less likely to lay down a 'word picture' of an event. Studies of memory in adults have shown that rehearsal makes it much more likely that an event will be remembered.

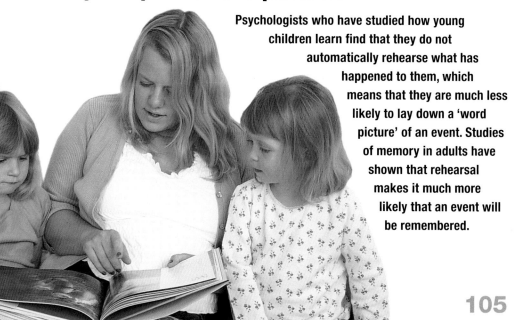

picture quiz
from 2 years

Use old magazines for this visual memory game.

- Tear out a few large pictures from some old magazines.

- Take one picture and look closely at it with your child for a minute or so. Then turn it over.

- Take turns to remember specific details about the picture. For example, you could say 'There was a girl and a boy in the picture'. Your child might add, 'The girl was wearing a blue dress', and so on.

- When neither of you can remember anything more, turn the picture back over to check how well you did.

funny people
from 3 years

Your child can create her own mix-and-match characters.

- Take a few pieces of paper, stack them, then fold them in half to make a 'book'.

- Holding the book at the fold, make two horizontal cuts across the middle, stopping short of the fold, dividing the book into three sections.

- On each page, draw a character, with the head in the top section, the body in the middle, and the legs at the bottom. You could draw a clown, a sailor, a fireman, a ballet dancer and a diver, for example.

- When the book is finished, ask your child to find some funny characters, for example, one with a fireman's head, a clown's body and a ballet dancer's legs.

106

RESEARCH SAYS

'Pile on the praise with visual memory games and see your child flourish.'

Research suggests that believing you can do something often means you'll succeed – even believing that you'll recover from an infection can influence how fast you recover. 'Pairs' is a game a small child can often play as well or better than an adult so playing it gives him lots of confidence. If children gradually build up competence with tasks like these, they're more likely to progress to more difficult problems believing 'I can'.

pairs
from 4 years

Use Snap cards or traditional playing cards to play this matching game.

- Lay all the cards face down on the floor.

- Let your child turn over any two cards to see if they match. If they do, he can keep the pair and turn over two more cards. If they don't, he must replace the cards where they were.

- Now, you turn over two cards – keep them if they match, put them back if they don't.

- Continue until all the cards have gone. The person with the most pairs wins.

- With younger children, use a smaller number of pairs.

looking at photographs

*photos give your child a sense
of his place in the family*

We all love photos, because they provide a visual record of our lives and because they so often bring back happy memories.

Building up a visual store of good, happy memories will help your child to look back on his childhood with pleasure. Try to take a camera with you whenever you go out for the day, to a family celebration or even to the park. As well as posed shots, try to take a few funny pictures as well – perhaps one of the baby with ice-cream all over his face, or the wind blowing Daddy's hair on end. You can guarantee these will be the favourites in years to come!

Your child will be particularly fascinated by pictures of himself as a baby. But as well as these, he'll love looking at photos of you

play and learn

baby talk

Find some photos of your child as a baby and talk about all the funny things babies do, such as drinking milk, crying and being sick! Remind your child of all the amazing things he can do now that he's a 'big boy', such as running, jumping and drawing pictures.

photo copying

Find a head-and-shoulders shot of someone in your family and ask your child to draw a copy of it, and make sure he looks very carefully at all the details, such as hair length, eye colour and clothes.

my soft toys

Take some photos of your child's favourite soft toys in different poses and make a special album to put them in when they've been developed. A fun way to do this is to put them in an unusual setting, such as sitting in a tree, or on an upturned flowerpot.

**'Try to take a camera
with you whenever you go out
for the day, to a family celebration
or even to the park.'**

and your partner as children. Not only will it give him a sense of family history, but it'll also help him to realize that you were young once and might be able to understand how he feels sometimes.

Photos are also great reminders of people that your child doesn't see every day, such as his grandparents. You could put a photo of Grandad in his room so that he can say goodnight to him at bed-time, or show him photos of absent uncles, aunts, cousins and friends. Pictures of pets are likely to be especially popular! And, of course, he'll feel extra proud if there's a picture of him on display, too – perhaps achieving a goal, such as riding his new bike.

Looking at baby photos together is also a great way of boosting your child's confidence, especially if he's feeling anxious about the arrival of a new baby or is having trouble adjusting to a new role as big brother. It gives you the opportunity to reinforce how big, grown-up and clever he is now and how the baby will look up to him in the future.

109

clothes muddle
from 2 years

Your child can exercise her memory while she's getting dressed.

- Lay out your child's clothes, but leave out one key item, such as her T-shirt or one sock.

- Tell her it's time to get dressed, but that she has to guess which item you've 'forgotten' to put out.

- As she puts on each item, encourage her to say its name, for example, 'That's right, first your... vest. Now, your... pants, and... shorts, then your... oh, have you guessed what's missing yet?'.

- When she has guessed, she could fetch the item from the drawer or cupboard herself.

unfinished pictures
from 2 years

Can your child spot what's not in the picture?

- Draw a picture of a familiar object, such as a bicycle, a house or a cat, but leave out an important detail. For example, the bicycle might have only one wheel or the house might be missing a door.

- Ask your child to look at the picture and tell you what detail is missing.

- As she improves at this game, make the missing items less obvious. For example, a teapot without a lid or a door without a handle.

- Older children can draw some pictures for you to guess what's missing.

what's gone?
from 4 years

This is similar to Kim's game (p. 101), but instead of taking away all the objects, you remove only one.

- Lay out ten small objects on the floor, such as a pencil, a key and an apple.

- Ask your child to close her eyes for a while.

- Remove one item and hide it behind your back.

- Ask your child to open her eyes and guess which object you've taken away.

- If she guesses incorrectly put the item back and play again, removing a different item this time; if she guesses correctly, take the item out from behind your back and congratulate her!

RESEARCH SAYS

'In order to tell you what is missing, a child must first tell herself what she can see.'

Doing so encourages her to 'talk to herself' and so put experiences into words. Studies of young children show that they do not automatically do this even when they are trying to remember – although their memory is always better if they do so.

RESEARCH SAYS

'These tasks encourage children to categorize to aid recall.'

If we are asked to remember a list of objects, we tend to remember them category-by-category – all the soft toys, then all the vehicles, for example. If we are presented with lists of words already in categories, we remember more words. Small children do not remember things by category even if the categories are obvious, and do not spontaneously make use of the categories to aid recall.

what's in your toybox?
from 2 years

Recall some familiar toys and favourite items.

- Start by focusing your child's attention on his toys. For example, you could say, 'You've got lots of lovely toys at home, haven't you, Ben?'

- Begin to list them for him, then ask him to add to your list. For example, 'There's Bunny, your train set, your farm, and... what else can you think of, Ben?'

- He may remember his toys without much prompting, but if he needs a clue, you could say 'Which toy has a blue waistcoat?' for example.

- Try other lists, such as the books on your child's shelf or the names of his friends.

categories
from 4 years

Take it in turns to build up a list of similar items.

- Ask your child to think of a category, such as types of sweets, children's TV characters, or even favourite dinners.

- Say you're going to take it in turns to think of as many things as you can within that category.

- Count how many items you've each thought of in a particular category to see which of you is the winner.

- For older children, make the categories more difficult, for example, flowers, countries or makes of car.

picnic party
from 5 years

Fill your basket with this fun alphabet memory game.

- Start the game by saying 'One day, we went to the beach and in our picnic basket we had some apricots.'.

- Your child then has to repeat the sentence and add a new item beginning with 'b', such as a 'beetroot'.

- Continue adding things to your picnic basket, taking it in turns and working your way through the alphabet.

- If you manage to get all the way to 'z', you deserve a big pat on the back!

113

memorizing personal details

remembering her address and phone number could be vital for your child

The best way for your child to learn her address is to memorize it in sections. Start by pointing out the name or number on your door and telling her what it is. You could say 'our house has a red door with a big letter-box and the number 28 on it – look, there are the numbers'. Hold your child up to have a good look at them and, if the numbers are raised, let her feel them.

Move on to learning the name of the road you live on. Point out the road name every time you pass it and explain that that's how people know it's your street. Then, refer to the name of your town when you're chatting together, and add it to the number and road. 'We live at 28, Park Crescent, Hustley – Hustley begins with a big "h", doesn't it?' Point out road or shop signs that include the name of your town when you're out and about.

Learning the postal code is the hardest part of memorizing a full address, and in all

> **'The best way for your child to learn her address is to memorize it in sections.'**

probability your child is unlikely to know this until she has been at school for a while. However, you can show her your postcode on an envelope and explain that it's how the postman knows which house to deliver your letters to.

Phone numbers are also complicated, and it's unlikely that your child will be able to remember such a long sequence much before she's at least 4 years old. Phone numbers can have up to 11 digits in them, so it will help your child to learn hers in smaller groups of figures. Many children find it easier to remember their phone numbers as a sort of sing-song sentence, however, so it may be helpful to set yours to a catchy little tune.

play and learn

'i'm lost' role-play	my house	dear bunny...
Take turns to be lost and act out what you would do. Pretend to be a policeman who needs to know your child's address and see if she can get it right. Remind her never to go out of the door if she gets separated from you in a shop and not to talk to strangers (except policemen).	Ask your child to draw a picture of your house – she might want to sit outside and draw it from life. When she has finished, write her address clearly underneath and stick it on the wall in her room.	Help your child to write some letters to her toys and make up some silly addresses for them, such as Mr Rabbit, 2 Toys Road, Pillow Town, Bedroomshire. This will reinforce the structure of addresses.

115

what we do
from 2 years

Use toys to recall and rehearse a familiar everyday routine.

- Play putting Teddy to bed, following the same routine as you use to put your child to bed.

- Ask your child what she needs to do first. Oh yes, give Teddy a bath.

- Help her pretend to give Teddy a bath, and then to clean his teeth.

- When Teddy is ready for bed, let your child 'read' him a story, give him a cuddle and tuck him in.

- Rehearse other regular routines, such as getting up in the morning, having a meal or going to playgroup.

all about me
from 3 years

Make a book about your child so that she can look back on her childhood.

- Take a few sheets of paper, stack them and fold them in half to make a 'book'. Add a coloured cover if you wish.

- Find some photos of your child as a baby and toddler and stick them into the book.

- Ask your child what she would like you to write under each photo as a caption, for example, 'when I was a baby, I wore a nappy'.

- Draw around one of your child's hands on one page, and around her foot on another.

- Finish off with a list of your child's favourite things, such as her favourite colour, food, toy and game.

'**Research suggests that babies start to imitate our actions in the first weeks of life.**'

'Mirror' neurones (brain cells) not only fire when we do something, but also when we watch someone else doing exactly the same thing. Scientists believe that these neurones underpin imitation. Copying other people, playing through everyday routines and rehearsing past experiences may be among the most natural ways for a small child to learn.

places I've been
from 4 years

Keep a record of special trips or events to keep the excitement alive.

● Every time you go on a trip, for example, to the zoo, a farm, or on holiday, collect a few mementoes to take home. For example, a tour guide, some postcards or a leaflet; or just some shells, leaves or bark.

● When you get home, stick the mementoes in a scrap-book with a big title page for each occasion and perhaps some family photos and a drawing or two.

● Put the scrap-book on your child's bookshelf and, every now and then, take it out to 'read' instead of reading her a story.

what a puzzle!

Children love a challenge
and doing a puzzle is a stimulating
and mind-expanding activity. Use the games
in this chapter to help your child learn about
colour, shape and size, how to match
objects, answer questions, solve riddles
and follow clues.

match the kite
from 2 years

Can your child match the colour pairs?

● On a large piece of paper, draw 11 diamond-shaped kites with long tails.

● Colour the kites in matching pairs, making sure they're not next to each other. Colour the final odd one in another colour.

● Ask your child to point to each matching pair or, if she's able, to draw a line connecting the two.

● When she has linked all the pairs, help her to name the colours and find the odd-one-out.

guess the colour
from 3 years

A simple, but popular, guessing game.

● Make a basic cardboard cube by drawing four squares down, plus a square on either side of the second square. As you cut out the shape, leave little tabs on the outside edges for easy sticking.

● Colour each square a different colour, then stick the cube together with glue or sticky tape.

● Ask your child to guess which colour will land face-up when she rolls the cube.

● Then, ask her to roll the cube and see if she is right.

● Take it in turns to roll the cube and get a point each time you guess the colour correctly.

RESEARCH SAYS

'Naming colours takes practice.'

At birth, the central area of visual receptors in the eye (the fovea) is immature, and because the receptors in this area (the cones) process colour, tiny babies have very poor colour vision. Toddlers see colours perfectly well, and can match and group them, but they still have to learn how to name them.

spinning colour circle
from 4 years

Show your child how to turn three colours into lots of spinning rings!

- Cut out a circle of card – you could draw round the base of a mug or a small plate.

- Using red, green and blue felt-tip pens, let your child randomly cover the circle with large spots of colour.

- Put some play dough under the card and push a small pencil through the centre.

- Remove the play dough and let your child use the pencil to spin the circle. As it goes round, she'll see rings of different colours appearing.

what is it?
from 2 years

Recognizing objects from their outlines is quite a challenge.

- On a piece of paper, draw several pairs of objects with distinctive outlines, such as teapots, jugs, saucepans, spoons and garden spades. Make sure the two halves of each pair are not next to each other.

- Draw in some details and colour one picture from each pair, but turn the other picture into a black silhouette.

- Ask your child to look at the pictures and see if he can spot which coloured picture matches which silhouette.

- Can he tell you which of the five objects you wouldn't find in a kitchen?

spot the shape
from 3 years

Play this spotting game while shopping in the supermarket.

- Tell your child you're thinking of a particular shape, for example, a circle.

- Ask him to look around and point out any objects nearby that make circles. He might suggest a round packet of cheese, the top of a tin, a sign in the aisle, or the coins in your purse.

- Count up how many circles he has seen. Then, ask him to look for squares, triangles or rectangles.

- With an older child, you can introduce the idea of spheres, cubes and cylinders.

RESEARCH SAYS

'The recognition of shape broadens reading skills.'

Educationalists all agree that tasks which encourage children to look for detail and to recognize the outlines of shapes help children to read. An adult usually reads by recognizing word shape, but when this fails, he or she deciphers the words from their component letters. To become a competent reader, a child must be able to recognize letters (detail) as well as the overall shape (outline) of words.

shape people
from 4 years

Can your child make a person from linking shapes?

- Draw a square and a rectangle for your child so that he knows exactly what they look like.

- Then, tell him you'd like him to draw you a robot using different-sized squares and rectangles only.

- When he has finished, can he count up how many squares and how many rectangles he has used to make his picture? Which shape did he use most?

- Ask him to draw some other shape people, such as a clown made of circles and ovals, or a witch made up of only triangles.

deciding what to wear

make getting dressed easier and more fun

To save time, prepare your child's clothes the night before and distract her by putting on a nursery rhyme tape and singing while you get her dressed. Three-year-olds usually have very clear ideas about what they want to wear, often involving a particular T-shirt or sweater with a favourite character or motif. An expensive way to side-step this problem is to buy two identical garments – one for wearing, the other for washing. Alternatively, offer a choice between two outfits, so that you can introduce an element of variety, but your child still feels in control.

From around three years, most children will be starting to dress themselves. Lay out your child's clothes in order on the bed so that she can work from one end to the other. Putting on clothes in the right order is a good practical sequencing task and will enable you to introduce ideas such as 'socks first, shoes second'.

'Putting on clothes
in the right order
is a good practical
sequencing task.'

Getting dressed also provides opportunities for discussion. Look through a window together and ask your child which outfit would be suitable for today's weather. Talk about the sorts of fabrics that clothes are made from – wool for her cardigan and canvas or leather for her shoes. Expand her vocabulary with interesting words such as 'stretchy', 'elasticated', or 'itchy'!

Before long, your child will be able to sort out her own outfit. Arrange her cupboards and drawers so that she can reach everything and knows where to find different items. On the front of each drawer or cupboard, you could stick a little picture or, if she's beginning to read, write a label. At night, show her how to put her dirty clothes in the laundry basket to be washed.

play and learn

teddy twin

Ask your child to dress her teddy or doll in an outfit matching her own. Even if she doesn't have exact mini-replicas of her own clothes, she can approximate by colour or style.

dressing by colour

Have a day in which your child has to dress herself in one colour only, such as red or green. Can she find enough clothes to do it? Make it more fun by pretending she's Little Red Riding Hood, or Hector Protector.

imagine an outfit

Pretend you are a different person, such as a ballerina, an astronaut, a diver or an ice-skater, and ask your child what special clothes she thinks you might need; in our examples, a tutu and ballet shoes, a space suit, flippers or ice-skates.

125

hidden pictures
from 3 years

A sweep of a paint-brush will reveal creatures – great and small!

- Using a clear wax candle, lightly draw a large outline of an elephant on a piece of paper. On a separate piece of paper, draw a small outline of a mouse.

- Tell your child that you have 'hidden' a big animal on one piece of paper and a small animal on the other.

- Let your child paint all over the pieces of paper. As she does so, the wax pictures will be revealed.

- Ask which is the big animal and which is the small.

- An older child will enjoy making and painting over her own secret wax picture.

RESEARCH SAYS

'**Most children have difficulty arranging things by size, until they are about five.**'

While blue is clearly blue, and five is the number of digits on one hand, big and small are relative categories. A big fly is an order of magnitude smaller than a small dog, and a little car is an order of magnitude bigger than a small shoe.

balloon pairs
from 4 years

Find the balloons of the same size.

- On a piece of card, draw five pairs of balloons, ranging in size from very big to very small.
- Cut them out and ask your child to colour each balloon a different colour.
- Shuffle the balloons and ask her if she can sort them out into pairs of the same size.
- When she has matched all the pairs, ask her to line up the balloons in order of size.

tall to small
from 5 years

Ask your child to line up her belongings in height order.

- Find several groups of objects that come in different sizes, such as plastic pots, books, buttons, toy dolls, coins and bricks.
- Ask your child if she can line up each group in a row, starting with the tallest and going down to the smallest.
- Talk about your own family – who is the tallest; who is the smallest; who is in the middle?
- Discuss things that start small and grow tall, such as a baby to an adult, or a tiny seed to a great big sunflower!

find one like mine
from 2 years

Match a selection of paired household objects.

- Find a selection of matching pairs, such as plastic bowls, napkins, crayons, hair slides and ribbons.

- Put them in a pile, then choose one item and hold it up in the air.

- Say to your child 'Can you find me another one like this?' and let her look through the pile.

- When she finds the right item, praise her and name the object by saying 'Well done, you found the crayon'.

- Let her put the pair beside her, then hold up the next item for her to match.

RESEARCH SAYS

'Matching exercises can develop reasoning skills.'

If you show a picture of a bird to a nine-month-old child, she is initially quite excited, but after a while she stops looking at the picture. If the picture then changes to a different bird, the child shows no interest because it is too similar to the previous picture. If it changes to a horse, however, interest returns. Although babies and young children can implicitly form loose categories, they still have difficulty in saying how or why they group things together. These games practise these skills.

is it the same?
from 3 years

Turn a card to see if two pictures match.

- Draw a grid of boxes (three rows and three columns) on a piece of paper and draw a small picture in each one.
- Draw the same pictures on a second piece of paper, but cut these into individual cards.
- Create a second grid and set of cards with different pictures.
- Give your child one of the pieces of paper, while you keep the other. Then, shuffle the cards, place them face-down on the floor and take turns to turn one over. If a card matches a picture on your sheet, place it over the top.
- The winner is the first person to cover all their pictures.

fantastic flags
from 4 years

Copy the patterns to match the flags.

- Fold a piece of paper in half. Open it out again and, on each side of the fold, draw four blank flags. Repeat with a second piece of paper.
- Keep one piece of paper and give the other to your child. Ask her to decorate the four flags to the left of the fold, but to leave the others empty.
- Do the same with your flags, then swap papers and copy each other's flags on the right-hand side.
- Talk about the imaginary countries your flags might belong to.

the way home

*turn a familiar journey into
a learning opportunity*

Start with the basics – roads are for cars and pavements are for people, so your child must always stop and wait for you when he gets to the kerb. Show by example the 'Stop, Look, Listen' strategy before crossing small roads, and always use pedestrian crossings on larger roads. Remind your child how fast cars can go and how long they take to stop, and tell him that he must never cross a road without an adult.

Whether you're walking or driving, point out landmarks to your child as you go. These could include parks, churches, stations, schools, shops and clock-towers. More personal landmarks are good to mention, too, such as the door of his friend's house, or the place where he once fell over!

Try describing your route out loud as you go, whether walking or in the car, so that your child gets used to hearing directions. For example, you could say 'At the top of

'**Remind your child how fast cars can go and how long they take to stop, and tell him that he must never cross a road without an adult.**'

our road we're going right – that's towards the station, isn't it, Ben? Then we'll go along by the railway for a bit and turn left at the bridge, and down the hill towards your nursery school'.

When you're confident your child knows a particular route, let him take the lead if you're walking, or tell you what's coming next if you're driving. If possible, show your child an alternative route occasionally, perhaps by going to Grandad's house via the shops or through the park instead of by the most direct route. This will help him to construct a mental map of his home area, which is not only good for developing his spatial awareness, but would also come in handy if he was ever to get lost.

play and learn

count your way

Ask your child to help you count how many lamp-posts, post-boxes or garden gates there are on a particular stretch of road as you walk along.

directions

Ask your child to draw a road map, following your directions. Start off with a long road going across the page (west to east). Add a smaller road going up to the top (north), and another to the bottom (south). Finally, add a few landmarks, like a bridge, a shop and a tree.

treasure map

On a piece of paper, draw an island with misty mountains, dark forests, treacherous marshes, sandy coves and rocky cliffs – all surrounded by sea. Ask your child to mark an 'x' where treasure is hidden. To make the map look worn and old, tear the edges roughly and rub the paper with an old teabag.

RESEARCH SAYS

'Consistent reasoning is a challenge for a small child.'

If you ask a small child why three objects (A, B and C) are in the same category, he will be able to give you a perfectly good reason why A goes with B. Research suggests, however, that if you then go on to ask him why B goes with C, he may give you a quite different, but equally sensible, answer. Until they can think about more than two things at a time, it is difficult for young children to keep a consistent story.

what a mix up!
from 2 years

Practice with sorting objects into groups will make it easier for your child to clean up after himself!

- Find some small toys, such as model animals, bricks, miniature vehicles and plastic dinosaurs and then mix them all up. Also find a few shoe-boxes or paper bags (not plastic).

- Ask your child if he can pick out all the bricks and put them in one box or bag for you.

- When all the bricks are together, tell him you have another box for all the toy vehicles and ask him if he can find those for you, too.

- Carry on until all the toys are sorted into different sets.

- You could categorize still further by, for example, sorting bricks by colour, shape or size, or animals into 'farm', 'jungle' and 'pet'.

tops and bottoms
from 3 years

Can your child put a lid on it?

- Find as many tins, boxes and plastic pots with matching lids as you can. Separate the containers and lids, then jumble them up inside a big basket or pillow-case.

- Add a couple of extra containers or lids that don't have a matching half.

- Give the basket or pillow-case to your child and tell him that you've got into a terrible muddle and need his help to match as many lids to containers as he can.

- When he has finished, ask him if he has found any that didn't match up.

what goes with what?
from 4 years

Spot the items that naturally link together.

- Tell your child you're going to say a word and you want him to think of another word to go with it. For example, you might say 'cup', and he might say 'saucer'.

- Ask if he can guess 'partner' words for some of the following words – toothbrush (toothpaste); lock (key); hairbrush (comb); pen (paper); socks (shoes); dustpan (brush) and bucket (spade).

- Try mother and baby pairs, too, such as 'cow' and 'calf'; 'cat' and 'kitten'; 'horse' and 'foal'; 'duck' and 'duckling'; and 'hen' and 'chick'.

who am I?
from 2 years

Guess the animal by its shape and movement.

- Tell your child that you are going to pretend to be an animal – can he guess which one you are?

- Using your hands as ears, make your body into the basic shape of an animal – for example, a dog, a cat, a sheep or a pig. If your child finds it difficult to guess, you could make the animal sound to go with it.

- Ask your child to pretend to be an animal for you to guess, too. Help him along by giving some suggestions, such as, a very small animal with a long tail (mouse), or a large one with a trunk (elephant).

twenty questions
from 4 years

This is a favourite 'yes-no' count-down game.

- Tell your child that you are going to think of an object and will tell him if it is 'animal', 'vegetable' or 'mineral' (you may have to explain these concepts).

- He has to guess what the object is by asking you up to 20 questions, to which you can only answer 'yes' or 'no'. Useful questions include 'Can I see it?', 'Is it bigger than me?' and 'Would I find it in my house?'.

- When he gets closer to guessing the object, he can ask a direct question, such as 'Are you thinking of a horse?'.

RESEARCH SAYS

'These activities provide your child with practice at trying to "see through someone else's eyes".'

A small child's fascination with hide-and-seek games begins in his first year. At this stage, he is busy working out whether objects exist if he cannot see them – by 14 months he knows that they do, but he has not yet learned that other people do not see exactly what he sees or feel what he feels.

secret pictures
from 4 years

Can your child follow your instructions and copy your picture exactly?

- On a piece of paper, draw a simple picture of a house – with four windows, a door, a roof and a chimney – and colour it in.

- Hold the picture so that your child can't see it. Then, describe the house you've drawn and ask your child to draw a similar one.

- When he has drawn it, describe how you've coloured in your house. For example, say 'The front door is blue' or 'The chimney has smoke coming out of it'.

- Finally, compare pictures to see how similar (or different) they are.

sorting the laundry

enjoy lessons from your washing basket!

Explain the process of sorting dirty washing to your child step-by-step. First you have to separate the colours – this means sorting the clothes into piles of dark and light, brightly coloured and pastel. Ask your child to help you to sort the colours and put her in charge of loading the machine. She can then pour in the powder and fabric conditioner and watch you set the control buttons. Point out that the different fabrics need different temperature settings and, if your machine has one, show her the dial to see the progress of the cycle.

When the clothes are washed, your child can help you to peg them on the line, or transfer them to the tumble dryer. And when they are dry, she can fold them with you, matching corners and putting together things that belong in pairs, such as socks or pillow-cases. Finally, she can sort out which items of clothing belong to which

> **'Ask your child to help you to sort the colours and put her in charge of loading the machine.'**

member of the family and make separate piles of clean clothes for each person. She can help you carry piles of clothes into the right bedrooms, and pass them to you to be put away in drawers or wardrobes.

What has your child learnt by doing this? Well, by initially sorting the clothes she has developed a better understanding of colours and shade; by loading the machine she may have gained some idea of weight and capacity; by pouring in the powder and conditioner and by folding the clothes she's practised measuring and hand–eye co-ordination; and by matching socks, she has learnt about pattern and size. Not bad for a morning's work!

play and learn

clothing categories

Ask your child to sort the clean clothes into different categories. For example, she could try putting together all the things we wear on the top half, such as T-shirts, shirts, jumpers, cardigans and sweaters, or all the night-clothes, such as pyjamas, night-dresses and dressing-gowns.

peg dolls

Find some old-fashioned wooden pegs (craft shops often have them) and make some peg dolls by drawing on faces and 'dressing' them in scraps of fabric, lace and ribbon. Your child could use them to hang out her clothes to dry on a sunny day.

toys' laundry

Set out a washing-up bowl of soapy water and let your child do her own mini-wash of toys' clothes. If you have room, a mini clothes line will also be very popular, as will mini pegs.

what is it?
from 2 years

Can your child use the clues to guess what you are thinking of?

- Imagine something that your child is familiar with, for example, a particular animal, a vehicle, a place or a toy.

- Tell your child you want him to guess what you are thinking of and are going to give him some clues. For example, for a bus you could start off by saying 'The thing I'm thinking of is a very large vehicle'.

- Keep giving increasingly specific clues, such as 'It carries lots of people', and 'It takes us to the shops', until your child guesses correctly.

from one to another
from 3 years

Your child must find all the objects to get the treasure.

- Wrap and hide a small piece of 'treasure', for example, a plastic dinosaur or a sticker book.

- Cut out six small cards from a piece of paper and draw a single household object on each. For example, you might choose a beaker, a comb, a toy, a colander, a newspaper and a rug.

- Find the real objects and put one (uncovered) in each room to lay a trail to the treasure. Beside each object, place a card showing the next thing to find.

- Give your child the picture of the first object and watch him follow the clues to the treasure.

RESEARCH SAYS

'**Removing or distorting familiar images encourages a child to use his imagination.**'

Small children are dominated by what they see and are not able to ignore visual evidence in favour of reason. They do not think about things logically until they are about six or seven years old. Riddles and treasure hunts, however, force children to think about the unseen, encouraging them to develop logical skills.

animal treasure hunt
from 4 years

Guess the animal to get to the next clue.

- Make twelve small cards. On six, draw three obvious parts of a familiar animal. For a pig, for example, draw some pointy ears, a snout and a curly tail; for a rabbit, you could draw long ears, whiskers and a bob-tail.

- On each of the other cards, draw a simple picture of the place in which the next clue can be found, for example, a table, a cushion, a coat peg, stairs, a bed and a bath.

- Distribute five of the animal cards around the house as clues and hide the treasure near the last one.

- Give your child the first animal card and ask him to guess the animal. If he gets it right, hand him a 'place' card to show him where to go next.

- Continue until your child is able to find the treasure.

get
moving

Physical activity is essential for every growing child, and the games in this chapter will give you lots of ideas for ways to keep children racing, chasing, and enjoying their own strength and fitness. Regular exercise helps them to eat, sleep and learn more effectively, so make time for a good run around each day.

can't catch me!

from 2 years

Burn off lots of energy with this easy game that is great fun for two or more.

- Decide who is going to be 'It' – you or your child.

- Whoever is 'It' counts to five to give the other person a chance to run away.

- Then 'It' tries to catch the other person. As soon as she does so, the other person becomes 'It'.

- Young children can play in the garden, but older children will probably need the open spaces of a park.

40-40 home

from 4 years

Fast and furious, this game works best with more than one child.

- Choose a starting point (or 'home'), such as a bush or a sweater on the ground, where the game will begin.

- The child who is 'It', closes her eyes and counts to twenty, giving the others a chance to run away and hide. When she's finished counting, she starts to chase the others.

- The hidden children must try to reach 'home' without being caught by whoever is 'It'.

- If a child is successful, she shouts, '40-40 Home!', as she touches the starting point; but if she's caught, then she's out.

RESEARCH SAYS

'Chasing games help to improve a child's spatial awareness.'

Rats who are not allowed to chase each other never learn to make a spatial map of their world, whereas those that play chasing and wrestling games, do. In humans, boys tend to play more of these games than girls do, and although the gender difference is not that great, on average, men have better spatial skills than women.

tiger, tiger
from 4 years

A climbing-frame chasing game for two.

- You need to be sure your child is confident of her climbing skills before you begin this game.

- Tell your child that you are a hungry tiger, and she must climb up the climbing frame to escape!

- Once she's safely out of reach, you can wander a little way off, grumbling that there's nothing to eat here.

- Your child can then come down carefully – but dash back up again as soon as the hungry tiger returns.

- If your child finds this game too scary, she can pretend to be a bird flying back to the top of her tree when a person walks past.

hippety-hop
from 3 years

Young children love pretending to be animals.

● Tell your child he is a bunny rabbit and you'd like him to hop all around.

● When you say, 'Stop, Bunny!', he must freeze and keep completely still.

● Then, ask him to be another animal, for example, a kangaroo that loves leaping.

● Continue with other animals. He could try being a slithering snake, a stork lifting his long legs through a pond, or a butterfly flitting from flower to flower.

cloud nine
from 3 years

Make the most of your child's fascination with balloons.

● Blow up a balloon and secure it firmly, telling your child that it's a little cloud that wants to stay high up in the sky above the ground.

● Ask your child to show you how long he can keep the balloon up in the air without it landing on the ground – he can use his head, hands, arms, feet or legs to keep it airborne.

● An older child will enjoy counting aloud as he pats or kicks the balloon upwards.

'Play-acting expands the mind.'

Until they are about four years old, children assume that we see what they see and experience what they experience. Pretending to be someone or something else helps them to 'look beyond themselves' and physically acting out reinforces this concept.

giddy-up!
from 4 years

There's lots of leaping and jumping in this imaginative game.

- Set up a little show-jumping arena for your child by putting sticks across up-turned flower-pots.

- Ask your child to think of a name for his imaginary pony, then he can set off around the course, jumping over each obstacle.

- You can pretend to be a TV commentator, 'And Ben is jumping so well today – just look how he got over that one! And it looks like a clear round. Yes! He's made it! Ben is the champion'.

- If your child finds the jumps too easy, make them a little higher by stacking the flower-pots or using garden chairs to support the sticks.

at the park

*learning can be as simple
as a walk in the park*

A good park will include lots of wide-open spaces as well as a playground with activities to suit all ages. It may also have a programme of events for children, particularly in the summer, so keep your eye on notice-boards.

Make the most of the park's size by encouraging your child to have a good run around – remember, she is far more likely to have fun doing this if you join in! Throwing and catching games encourage social as well as physical skills, so it's well worth taking a small, soft ball with you. Don't forget that girls will enjoy a kick-around just as much as boys!

Many parks offer lots of opportunities to learn about nature and wildlife. If you're regular visitors, you can enjoy watching how the landscape changes with the seasons. You could collect small items, such as grasses, seeds, leaves and nuts, to make a seasonal display at home, though talk about the importance of not eating

'A park playground offers your child more exciting physical challenges than being at home does.'

berries. Children enjoy seeing animals close-up, and will love watching ducks, squirrels, birds and insects. Can your child guess where each one lives, and how they might react if you went up close to them?

A park playground offers your child more exciting physical challenges than being at home does. Swings, slides, climbing-frames and see-saws all help to improve co-ordination and strength. A vigorous outing that uses lots of energy gives your child the exercise she needs, so she's more likely to eat well and sleep soundly at night.

A nearby park is also an excellent place for making friends with other local parents and children.

play and learn

mini sports day

Take some basic items to the park and have a sports day of your own. Hold races such as a 'potato-and-spoon race' where you run along balancing a potato on a dessertspoon. Or try the 'low-down race', in which you have to make it to the finish line – while holding on to your ankles!

ball in a blanket

A great game if you're in the park with two children. Take a small blanket (a cot blanket is ideal) and a ball. The children each hold one side of the blanket, then you throw the ball and they have to try to catch it in the blanket. Take turns to be the ball-thrower.

goalie

Set up a nice wide 'goal' area, using sweaters, twigs or pebbles to mark its boundaries. Then, guard the entrance while your child boots the ball past you! Swap places and be sure to offer your little goalie some easy saves.

RESEARCH SAYS

'Bat-and-ball games enhance movement accuracy.'

Where in the brain do we plan actions such as positioning a bat to hit a ball? The frontal cortex (just below and to the front of the skull) initiates action and controls that action as long as we need to check a movement is correct, while the cerebellum (at the base of the brain) controls movements once they are flowing and skilled. If we spy on the brain by recording brain activity as people do things, we find that the cerebellum is also active when people are making plans.

first ball play
from 2½ years

Use a large, soft ball to practise his kicking, catching and throwing.

● Stand a few feet away from your child, and take turns to kick the ball towards each other. Gradually move further and further apart and see if you can still target each other accurately!

● From the age of three, your child can start to catch the ball by holding out his arms in front of him. Encourage him to keep looking at the ball (rather than you) as you throw it, and to clutch the ball to his chest, so that he doesn't drop it.

● Under-arm throwing is the best way for little children to start. Set up a row of skittles for him to knock over, or see if he can throw the ball into a bucket.

big hitter
from 4 years

Encourage bat-and-ball skills from an early age.

- Give your child a plastic bat, or make one by rolling up a newspaper and securing it with sticky tape.

- Using a small, soft ball, pitch under-arm to your child and see if he can hit the ball (you may need to use a bigger ball if he finds this too difficult).

- If he manages to hit the ball, let him do some cricket 'runs' back and forth, or run round four bases, as in rounders, while you collect the ball!

- Then, let him pitch the ball to you.

round the clock
from 5 years

Bouncing and catching games that your child can play by himself or that you can play together.

- Ask your child to bounce the ball once, then catch it.

- Next, let him try to bounce the ball twice before catching it.

- Continue the game, bouncing the ball three, four, five times and so on – right up to 12, if he can!

- Once your child is able to catch a bouncing ball, you could try bouncing the ball between the two of you.

- Make sure you are standing very close together to begin with, then gradually widen the gap.

keeping active when it's wet

*rain, rain,
don't go away!*

Swimming is a great way to have fun and keep active. Even if your child can't swim yet, you can help build her water confidence by singing rhymes such as Humpty Dumpty, encouraging her to jump in as you hold her securely; using floats to give her rides; and catching her as she splashes down a slide.

Explore some of the many clubs and classes available for children. For example, a preschool gym class will give her lots of opportunities to climb, stretch and jump about with other children, and you can be sure that the equipment is all designed to challenge her skills in safe surroundings.

At home, you could enjoy a mini disco session together, putting on some favourite music and dancing the afternoon away. You could have a mini exercise class in your sitting-room. Get your child to do on-the-spot jumps, star jumps or even skipping, to tire her out. A wet day is also a great opportunity to try some hide-and-

> **'You could have
> a mini exercise class
> in your sitting-room.'**

seek or treasure hunt games. These entail searching all around the house and will keep your child active and busy at the same time.

If you're both feeling really fed up with staying in, why not decide to brave the weather and go out anyway? Put on your water-proofs, hats and boots, and go out for a splashy walk, talking about which animals love water and rain, and which prefer the sunshine. Look at the wonderful patterns raindrops make as they hit puddles, and talk about the colour of the sky when it's full of rainclouds. Then, when you get home, you can dry off, cuddle up and watch a favourite video with a clear conscience!

play and learn

raindrop races

Sit together at a window watching the rain come down. Each of you must choose a raindrop that's landed at the top of the window at the same time, then follow its progress down the pane. The winner is the first raindrop to reach the bottom!

hide-and-seek

Close your eyes and count to 20, giving your child enough time to hide some-where in the room or the house. Then say 'Coming! Ready or not!' and seek her out. You could vary the game by giving animal noise clues as to your whereabouts.

stepping-stones

Put two pieces of paper on the floor and ask your child to stand on one. She then has to get across the floor by moving the pieces of paper forward and then stepping onto them one-by-one. She mustn't move the papers while her feet are on them.

151

grandmother's footsteps
from 3 years

A game of suspense and surprise.

- You are 'Grandmother', and stand facing the wall with your back turned. Your child stands at the other end of the room.

- He must creep up on you without making a noise.

- You can turn suddenly at any time, and your child then has to freeze and stand still.

- If you see him move, he must go back to the start, but if he reaches you, he can tap you on the back saying, 'Hello, Grandmother!'

- Swap places, so that your child is Grandmother.

wheelbarrows
from 4 years

This game requires a lot of strength and co-ordination.

- Choose a soft surface, such as grass, and ask your child to lie face-down on his tummy on the ground, with his legs straight.

- Take hold of his ankles and lift them, while he pushes down until his arms are straight.

- Set off, with your child walking along on his hands, while you support his 'wheelbarrow' legs. How many steps can you manage before collapsing in giggles?

- This could be fun played as a race with several other adult-and-child teams but make sure the ground is clear of any stones or obstacles first.

RESEARCH SAYS

'Some games exercise skills derived from primitive survival needs.'

Some scientists believe that a human's large brain and high level of intelligence arose because of his need to out-smart predators. The ability to deceive others is key to these games. It is often an advantage for us to fool people into thinking we are going to do one thing, while we are really planning to do another.

simon says
from 4 years

Movement, action and fun, all in one.

- Explain to your child that you want him to copy the actions you do, but only if you first give the instruction 'Simon says...'. For example, if you say 'Simon says... put your hands in the air', he must put his hands in the air, but if you just say 'Put your hands in the air', he should keep still.

- If he copies an action when you haven't said, 'Simon says', then he's out.

- To make the game livelier, give some more energetic movement instructions, such as 'Simon says... hop around the tree', or 'Simon says... skip all the way to the gate and back'.

treasure seeker
from 3 years

A relay-style game to encourage lots of running.

- Set out four or five different-coloured bricks or different toys in a row – these are the treasure items.
- Move to the other side of the room, and ask your child to be a treasure seeker who has found exciting things.
- Ask her, for example, 'Find the red brick' and she must run to get it and bring it back to put in your bag. Then, name the next item she has to get, and continue until they've all been collected.
- To vary the game, your child could pretend to be a dog fetching sticks or a mouse collecting food for winter.

stopwatch races
from 4 years

Let your child enjoy being a record-breaker!

- Mark the 'start' and 'finish' lines for a running track in your garden or the park.
- Using a stopwatch, or just the second hand of your watch, time your child as she runs from the start to the finish line.
- After a rest, let her have another go and see if she can improve on her previous time.
- Liven up the race by creating obstacles, for example, your child could run twice round a bush and jump over the path during the race.

spell my name
from 5 years

Let your child show you how clever she is by writing in footsteps!

- On a piece of paper, help your child to practise writing her name.

- When she's really confident of all the letters, see if she can write her name by pacing it out in footsteps. If this is too difficult, she could just do the initial letter.

- Vary the size – she could pace out a giant letter, or take tiny steps to make it very small.

- This is particularly rewarding when your child can see an imprint of her name, for example, in sand, snow or even mud!

RESEARCH SAYS

'Social and physical activities could be cortex-building.'

It is certainly true that the 'higher' centre of the brain (the cerebral cortex, which controls perception, action, learning and memory) is bigger in social species than in non-social species. It is also true that a rat raised in solitary confinement has a much thinner cerebral cortex than a rat raised in a social environment. One of the things that solitary rats miss out on is running and chasing games, which could be an indication that running and chasing are cortex-building activities.

playing together

*being able to share and take turns are
essential for your child to enjoy games with others*

**If your child goes to nursery
school, or to a child minder
during the day, he'll already be
used to getting along with
others, but if he's at home, make
sure he has opportunities to
meet up with children his own
age, by inviting friends over, and
visiting them at home.**

If he's shy and finds it hard to join in, you
could suggest some simple ways to start a
conversation, such as, 'Hello, I'm Ben.
Would you like to play?' You may need to
stay with him while he starts to play with
another child, gently encouraging a game,
but ready to fade into the background once
they're settled.

Help him to understand the concept and
importance of sharing and taking turns by
playing games with him at home that
emphasize these skills, for example,
organize a pretend picnic, in which you
pass each other food; or simple card
games, such as Snap, in which taking
turns is essential.

'Young children can be frustrated by the idea of rules in a game and may get cross when they don't win.'

Young children can be frustrated by the idea of rules in a game and may get cross when they don't win. Explain how important it is to follow the rules so that it's fair for everyone playing – especially if your child is in a group at a party or playgroup.

You'll need to be on hand to supervise any team games for preschool children, as rules will need to be explained several times before they really understand. The very best way to get the message across is by demonstration – so be prepared to do some racing, chasing and catching.

The best reward for children who've played co-operatively is for you to notice how good they've been, and praise their behaviour. Everyone likes a pat on the back!

play and learn

stuck-in-the-mud

One child is 'It', and has to try to catch the others, who all run around in an open space. Anyone caught has to stand still, feet apart 'stuck in the mud'. He can be rescued by any other player crawling between his legs, and is then able to run off again. The last child left unstuck is 'It' next time.

relay race

Divide the children into equal teams, giving each team a baton. Each team member has to run to a specified place, touch it with the baton, then run back and pass the baton to the next team member, who runs off to do the same thing. The first team to complete the race wins.

my ball, your ball

The children stand in a circle. Whoever has the ball says the name of another child and throws the ball to them. If they catch it, they can call another child's name and throw the ball; if not, they pass it to the child next to them. Stand the children close together to make it easier; further apart to make it harder. Suit the ball size to their abilities.

obstacle course
from 2 years

Clamber and climb over everyday things.

- Find a selection of items such as cushions, rugs, chairs, cardboard boxes, a hoop and a blanket.

- Create a mini-gym by arranging them around the room and let your child have fun climbing over, under and around the obstacles.

- You could also arrange cushion 'stepping-stones' that your child has to use to get from obstacle to obstacle.

- This is fun in the garden, too, where you can create a bigger course, and you could time an older child to see how quickly she gets around it.

do the conga
from 3 years

Dance is one of the most enjoyable – and easiest – forms of exercise.

- Put on some up-beat music and tell your child you're going to follow a dance path, for example, from the front door to the sitting-room and back, and you'd like her to dance after you, imitating whatever you do.

- Vary your movements as you go. Try waving your arms in the air, kicking out sideways like a conga, crouching down, or doing skipping steps.

- Let your child have a turn at leading the way. She can then choose funny dance movements for you to imitate.

RESEARCH SAYS

'Sharing games like these help to secure positive social attachments.'

We are a social species and research suggests that our health and happiness are tied to the provision of our social needs. This is particularly true for small children, who flourish in warm and loving environments. Research shows that children who have formed secure attachments to their parents are more likely to succeed in life.

catching forfeits
from 5 years

A catching game to challenge your child's hand–eye co-ordination.

● Practise throwing and catching a soft ball together. Once you have both warmed up, introduce forfeits for each time you miss a catch.

● The first miss means you have to kneel on one knee; a second means you have to kneel on both knees; a third means you have to put one arm behind your back; and a fourth means you have to lie on your back and try to catch the ball with one hand!

● To play the game with a younger child, you'll need to make your throws easy to catch, so stay close to her and use a medium-sized ball.

index